RAISING
EMPOWERED CHILDREN

RAISING
EMPOWERED
CHILDREN

THE CODEPENDENT PERFECTIONIST'S GUIDE TO PARENTING

ALANA CARVALHO

DOWNTOWN
Publishing

Copyright © 2020 Alana Carvalho
All rights reserved.

No part of this book may be reproduced, or stored in a retrieval system, or transmitted in any form or by any means, electronic, mechanical, photocopying, recording, or otherwise, without express written permission of the publisher.

Published by Downtown Publishing

Edited and designed by Girl Friday Productions
www.girlfridayproductions.com

Edited by Mary Hoekstra
Cover design by Paul Barrett
Project management by Alexander Rigby

ISBN-13: 978-1-7345348-0-1

To my daughters, Raquel and Chloe. May you believe in yourself, feel empowered, and always know your greatness.

CONTENTS

Introduction 1

Chapter 1: Codependency 5
Chapter 2: Perfectionism 23
Chapter 3: You Don't Own Your Children 37
Chapter 4: Transitional Parenting 51
Chapter 5: How to Be There 59
Chapter 6: Take a Step Back 71
Chapter 7: Consequences & Boundaries 77
Chapter 8: Navigating Your Power 93
Chapter 9: Age-Appropriate Behavior 101
Chapter 10: Positive Reinforcement 111
Chapter 11: Role Modeling 117
Chapter 12: Break the Cycle 125
Chapter 13: Clarity & Communication 131
Chapter 14: Holding Space & Listening 141
Chapter 15: Allowing for ALL Emotions 147

Chapter 16: How to Love Our Kids 157
Chapter 17: Is It Really All about Them? 165
Chapter 18: Being Perfectly Imperfect 173
Chapter 19: Parenting As a Spiritual Act 179

Acknowledgments 183
Bibliography 185
About the Author 191

INTRODUCTION

As I write this book, the US is in the thick of a suicide epidemic. Anxiety, stress, and depression are all on the rise. The pain we are experiencing as humans in the modern age is serious. As a licensed mental health counselor with a private practice in New York City, I work with a lot of people who are struggling in their own pain. Many of them are fearful of the gravity of bringing a child into this world. They worry whether they can be good parents and help a child navigate the complexities of life. My answer to this is *It's all about healing* you.

Working with hundreds of clients to help them heal their childhood trauma, past emotional wounds, and adult relationship issues has given me deep insight into the type of experiences that can have a big impact on how someone parents their own children. In my practice, I guide people toward conscious parenting and raising empowered children. Being a conscious parent means being aware—aware of yourself, aware of the unique needs of your child, and aware of the difference between your issues and your child's. Being a conscious parent means raising empowered children who can trust themselves and thrive in the world.

Parenting is tough. We are given charge of another human with little to no understanding of how to care for a child, and, more often than not, we just repeat what we know from our own parents and family life. As parents, we have the ability to do so much more than just repeat the past. We have the power to impact our children in so many ways, both positive and negative. With awareness of our past and who we really are, we have the ability to influence our children in many positive ways so they can function more effectively in this crazy world.

As adults, if we don't work on our own trauma and understand how it shapes who we are today, we'll likely go one of two ways when we become parents: we either recreate our past hurts, or we try to run from them and do the opposite. Both ways are *reactions* to our past rather than authentic representations of the present. When we have children, we unconsciously project our fears, hopes, and dreams onto them. My hope for you is that this book will help you explore how to consciously parent so your kids don't have to go through many of the same negative experiences you had. I offer an approach to parenting that provides children with the utmost growth possible, free from reactivity of our old pain and trauma.

I focus on two dynamics that I've observed within most of the parents I counsel. I've identified these issues as unique in their ability to prevent true connection between parent and child and perpetuate negative family cycles. And I should know, because I have struggled with both for my entire life. These dynamics are codependency and perfectionism. Codependency is defined here as relational and emotional enmeshment or the need for others to be OK in order for oneself to be OK. Perfectionism is an extreme need to appear flawless as well as a belief that one should strive to be the best (at all times). These tendencies present themselves to varying degrees within individuals and families, but they often work together to keep parents stuck in unrewarding and ineffective habits.

Codependency and perfectionism are family dynamics that become generational trauma when not worked through and healed. This book is here to help you break the cycle. *Raising Empowered Children: The Codependent Perfectionist's Guide to Parenting* provides you with a framework for understanding your own pain and how to successfully raise your children in a safe and loving environment full of connection and free from the grips of codependency and perfectionism.

The book consists of a mix of psychoeducation, personal anecdotes, therapeutic knowledge, and client case studies. I approach the material from my experience as a mental health professional as well as a human and a parent working through codependency and perfectionism myself. Throughout the chapters, we cover topics like how to communicate effectively with your children in a way that encourages them to feel heard, seen, and accepted; how to both be in a position of power as the parent as well as raise children who feel empowered; and how to achieve a spiritual understanding of why we have the children we do. I also include reflective exercises at the end of each chapter to help you apply the concepts and strategies to your own experience.

Something else that inspired me to write this is that it's very difficult for parents in our modern society to get support. I want this book to provide support throughout your parenting journey. I also encourage you to seek out additional support through things like parent groups, therapy, friends, and family. None of us can do this alone—and we shouldn't. So, don't be shy about asking for help when you need it. Codependents and perfectionists tend to have a hard time asking for and receiving support, but it's essential for our own well-being and therefore the well-being of our children.

In full transparency, I was very tough on parents before becoming a parent myself. Although I had a lot of knowledge on what it meant to be a helpful, loving, empathetic parent, I really didn't understand what it actually took physically, emotionally, spiritually, mentally, and energetically until I had a child. I couldn't relate to the complex difficulties that arise in everyday life with children. I have significantly softened my language and approach as a result of my own experience. I have so much empathy yet still hold parents responsible for their actions and how they impact their children. We are ultimately responsible for how we raise and impact our children. Owning our struggles and flaws is part of the process. Doing so proactively will allow us to raise empowered children who can do the same.

There is no greater gift we can give our children than to work on ourselves and end dysfunctional family patterns. Some patterns may be as simple as not speaking about negative emotions, and some may involve deeply complex trauma. Either way, I hope you find this book helpful in beginning your journey of healing and finding a better way. I wish you a voyage filled with growth into yourself as you become the best parent you can be.

CHAPTER 1

CODEPENDENCY

My therapist leaned toward me in our first session and asked, "Who are you?"

I had no idea how to answer. I instantly had a flashback to college, when one of my favorite professors had asked me a similar question. I remember the clear disappointment on his face when I couldn't come up with an answer. He couldn't believe that I—a stellar student in his consumer behaviorism class, someone who was always able to identify and express who other people were, break down difficult human dynamics, and analyze how society worked—couldn't explain who I was.

When I finally answered my therapist, we both noticed that I defined who I was based on *who I was to other people*: daughter, sister, friend, therapist, and student. Looking back, I really feel for that younger me, who was lost and operating as a shell of herself. That person could only define herself in relation to others' needs and expectations.

I've come to realize and believe wholeheartedly that we come into this world as perfect souls on a journey that we sign up for, knowing that this journey will take us away from our soul, or true self. On the journey of life, we are impacted by our family system, our culture, our society's values, our religious upbringing, and all our varied life experiences. These influences—combined with genetics—determine who we become. Unfortunately, this means we grow away from who we came into the world being. I didn't come into this world codependent, but I did walk into my therapist's office as a fully codependent young woman.

Codependency is a word that gets tossed around a lot these days. But what exactly does it mean? Originally, codependency was primarily discussed in relation to substance abuse and addiction. In her groundbreaking book *Codependent No More*, Melody Beattie coined the term for the mainstream recovery audience and helped readers understand and sort through their codependent patterns. According to her definition, "a codependent person is one who has let another person's behavior affect him or her, and who is obsessed with controlling that person's behavior." In relation to substance abuse, the desire to fix, change, or protect the substance abuser often results in enabling them. This destructive relationship pattern is considered codependency.

The idea of codependency has evolved over time. Although it definitely still applies in relation to addiction, I like to think of codependency as simply *emotional and relational enmeshment*. This can happen in many different types of relationships—not just those with an addict. It's like an invisible string tied to someone else that impacts how we feel, the choices we make in our life, and our identity. The codependent person says, "I'm only OK if you're OK" and bases their emotional state on the emotional state of someone else.

Codependency is a learned behavior that can be deeply ingrained by the time we become adults. Consider the last time you wanted someone to act differently. Maybe you believe that your brother should be kinder to you, or your child should listen to your advice. (I find that the thought *should* is always an indicator of where we may be trying to control someone else!) However, we can't simultaneously accept someone *and* believe they should be different. These are subtle ways codependency can manifest and create strife in relationships, negatively impacting both parties. Throughout the book, we'll continue to explore all the ways codependency can manifest, particularly when it comes to parenting.

Codependency is generally created in the early years of life from a mix of the following: learned behavior from parents, trauma, birth order, narcissistic parenting, addiction in the family, personality predisposition, genetic predisposition, and being an empathic being. As we address codependent parenting and how it can negatively shape our children and family dynamics, it's good to get an idea of where your own codependency comes from as the parent.

IMPACT OF TRAUMA

In my experience as a therapist, I observe that codependency is most strongly connected with childhood upbringing and trauma. You may be thinking, *Well,* my *childhood wasn't traumatic!* Mine wasn't particularly either, but I still had loads of experiences that impacted me strongly in ways than can be considered traumatic. Unfortunately, all humans will experience pain and trauma, large and small. As Americans, we understand poverty as trauma. We understand sexual assault as trauma. We understand being in a war-torn country as trauma. What we don't understand is that simply being human may also be traumatic. No family is perfect. No childhood is perfect. In fact, often the childhoods that look the "best" are filled with pervasive emotional trauma stemming from all the things we don't discuss in our culture, such as emotional neglect.

As a result of this, many of my clients don't understand why they are struggling and start off by saying, *But my childhood was perfectly normal!* or *My parents were good people; they didn't do anything harmful!* when it's likely that they experienced some sort of emotional trauma that is connected with their being codependent as adults and parents.

In my practice I tend to work with people whose trauma is not obvious yet is often complicated. These are people whose lives look perfect on paper—they have a solid family life, a good education, and plenty of resources and opportunity. But I know that's never the whole story. Our culture tends to assume that someone with a "good" upbringing or childhood will have no pain or problems. We are too quick to dismiss the kind of trauma that this type of person may have experienced. But trust me: Trauma within a "good" upbringing and a well-to-do lifestyle can be more insidious than an externally obvious trauma, as well as being highly debilitating if not treated.

> Deshawn was raised in an upper middle-class household with two married parents. By the looks of it, Deshawn's upbringing was very good. He grew up in a nice neighborhood in the suburbs of Chicago, attending a good primary school and having all his basic needs met and more. His parents were both professionals who valued school and hard work. When I met Deshawn, it was obvious to me that he was intelligent and got along well with others. Deshawn came to see me after struggling with a marijuana addiction for eight years. During this

time, he lived in his parents' basement and was mostly unemployed and not in school. Deshawn dropped out of college at some point when his marijuana addiction really flared up. When I met Deshawn, he had just stopped using marijuana and was highly apathetic about his life. He had no motivation to get a job or go back to school. Much of my work with Deshawn centered on healing the nonobvious trauma he had experienced throughout his upbringing by having two parents from whom he felt disconnected. Deshawn believed his parents cared more about school and work than they did about him and who he was. Ultimately, this left him feeling unloved and unseen. Not surprisingly, Deshawn became apathetic about these parts of his life, sabotaging his ability to succeed at them. It's almost as if he was saying to his parents, *Will you still love me if I don't succeed?* Throughout his time in counseling, our work centered on Deshawn healing his emotional wounds as well as working on loving himself enough to engage in his life. Deshawn slowly began to care and to love himself, eventually going back to school and getting a job because *he* wanted to, not because of his parents' need for him to.

Another way we can be impacted as children is by our parents' unhealed wounds and traumas. Many of us codependents come from generations of codependents before us. Our own parents have experienced their own trauma from having codependent parents and sadly have passed this down to us! Not on purpose, of course. John Bradshaw does a good job of exploring the pain of being raised by wounded people in his book *Home Coming: Reclaiming and Championing Your Inner Child* (1990). He explains how our parents' trauma impacts us and creates our own trauma, which we then pass on to our children unless we heal and break the cycle.

HOW DO I KNOW IF I AM CODEPENDENT?

Here are some questions to consider to help you identify your own codependency:

- Do you have trouble feeling OK if someone around you is not?
- Do you feel the need to fix or change other people's feelings or circumstances when you're uncomfortable with what they're experiencing?
- If you know someone may be hurt or reactive to something that you want to share, do you choose not to share it? Do you omit important details to avoid causing someone else to feel upset?
- Do you immediately try to give advice or help another see the positive when they share an issue they are struggling with?
- Do you have trouble being honest if it means disappointing someone else?
- Do you avoid conversation that may be considered "difficult" or "challenging"?
- Do you avoid putting boundaries in place with people for fear of how they might feel or react?
- Do you avoid expressing your needs or wants clearly to others?
- Do you feel resentment for how others treat you?
- Do you do more than your fair share because you assume or believe others won't pick up the slack?
- Do you worry excessively about others and what they're going through?

- Do you obsess about people in your life and how they're feeling?
- Do you feel obligated to take part in activities or relationships that you don't want to participate in?
- Do you have trouble saying no?
- Do you feel that other people's feelings are your responsibility to fix or change?
- When someone tells you about their negative experiences, do you immediately feel the need to give advice, make suggestions, or try to get them to do something differently?
- Do you have trouble asserting yourself?
- Do you bend to others' wishes even when it's something you really don't want?
- Do you feel the need to respond to people immediately when they contact you?
- Do you have trouble speaking up at work to ask for a raise or changes that feel important to you?
- Do you have trouble identifying what your needs are?
- Do you feel other people are in some way more important or more intelligent or capable than you?
- Do you prioritize other people over yourself?
- Are you underpaid and overworked?
- Do you avoid letting people know when you're upset or angry with them?
- Do you have a hard time knowing when people are upset with you?

Count how many you answered yes to. If you answered yes to one to four questions, you may have some minor codependent tendencies but are not fully codependent with others. If you answered yes to five to ten questions, you have moderate codependency issues. If you answered yes to ten or more questions, you've got more serious codependency issues. Keep that in mind as we continue to explore codependency further.

Many people ask me, "Alana, don't you think everyone is codependent?" And my answer is yes, to some degree. We live in a society that reinforces codependent and addictive tendencies. However, we don't all have them to the same degree. And therefore it will show up differently for all of us.

THE CODEPENDENT DYNAMIC

Codependency can be complicated. I find it's best to explore it as a dynamic with the issue of control at its core. The codependent person wants to control someone else because of how that person's behavior, feelings, and experiences impact them. We try to control the other person in hopes of controlling our own emotional state and reactions. For example, you don't want Joe to feel sad because it makes you feel sad, so you try to change Joe and his experience. This is what enmeshment looks like, where we have trouble separating our feelings from someone else's. Getting out of the codependent dynamic means allowing Joe to feel sad and instead working on your own experience of Joe's sadness.

As parents, it's especially easy for us to enmesh into our children's experience and try to get them not to feel any negative feelings because of how it makes *us* feel. But this is actually damaging because it sends the message to our children not to feel these feelings. Our children can have a range of reactions based on this experience, including bringing their emotions underground. Bringing their emotions underground means repressing or disconnecting from their true emotional experience, which is not healthy for their wellness and development. We want our children to learn to experience and work through their emotions, not repress them. Repression can lead to serious issues such as substance abuse and other addictions, eating disorders, and other mental health struggles.

Codependents often have a very limited idea of who they are and utilize other people and experiences in order to define themselves. For example, I often used to introduce myself as "Danielle's sister" instead of as "Alana," as if that was somehow more indicative of who I was. It's common to see codependents obsessing about not wanting to let others down or let them feel bad. It's often said that codependents have trouble knowing *where they end and where another person begins.* The only way to work on correcting this dynamic is to become aware of it in yourself and how it affects your behavior. Only then can you relinquish control over another person and find a healthy balance in your relationship.

Codependency can be highly debilitating and can manifest in every area of life from family to work. Pia Mellody gives a wonderful understanding of five core aspects of codependency in her book *Facing Codependence* (1989). She writes that codependents have trouble in the following areas. See if any of these resonate with you.

CORE SYMPTOMS OF CODEPENDENCY AS DEFINED BY PIA MELLODY (1989):

Area 1: Difficulty Experiencing Appropriate Levels of Self-Esteem

Area 2: Difficulty Setting Functional Boundaries: A personal boundary system is an internal mechanism that protects as well as contains an individual's body, mind, emotions, and behavior. It has three purposes:

1. To keep people from coming into our space and abusing us
2. To keep us from going into the space of others and abusing them
3. To give each of us a way to embody our sense of who we are

Area 3: Difficulty Owning Our Own Reality: People who are codependent do not know who they are. They have difficulty recognizing and defining their own reality. Reality is defined as the following four aspects:

1. The body—How we look and how our bodies are operating
2. Thinking—How we give meaning to incoming data
3. Feelings—Appropriate expression of our emotions
4. Behavior—What we do or don't do

Area 4: Difficulty Acknowledging and Meeting Our Own Wants and Needs: Everyone has basic needs and individual wants. Children must have their needs met initially by their primary caregivers. Then they must be taught to satisfy those needs themselves. Adults are responsible for addressing their own needs and asking for help when it is necessary. People who have difficulty with this can fall into these four categories:

1. Too dependent: We expect others to meet our needs completely
2. Anti-dependent: I alone can meet my needs

3. Needless/wantless: I am not aware of my needs or wants
4. Confuses wants and needs: Attempts to meet needs with wants (buying clothes instead of asking for physical intimacy)

Area 5: Difficulty Experiencing and Expressing Our Reality Moderately: This symptom is usually most visible to other people. Codependents usually have no middle ground and appear to be extreme with their bodies, thoughts, and feelings.

I relate to most of these characteristics. For the majority of my life I couldn't identify who I was and sometimes even what I felt. I often considered others' needs above my own and then resented them for not meeting my needs. My desire to "fix" others and make sure they were OK was at times overwhelming and all-consuming. I needed other people to be OK for me to be OK. Codependents are often thought of as wonderful caretakers, without consideration for the fact that we may be harming ourselves in our desire to always take care of others. We don't tend to identify what we need to make sure we're OK before we give to others. As the saying goes, we can't give from an empty cup. And so, as parents, we want to be careful about giving too much to our children and leaving our cup empty—this can breed all sorts of resentment over time.

CODEPENDENCY: SELFLESS OR SELFISH?

While it's well documented that addicts are selfish and tend to consider themselves above others, codependents are the opposite and tend to operate in a selfless way, considering others above themselves. This is why the addict (or narcissist)/codependent dynamic is so harmful. Codependents will take the shirt off their back for someone else, even when it's freezing out and they really need that shirt. They will contort themselves to make others happy and "not rock the boat," even if that leads to perpetuating the harmful behaviors and addictions of others.

But at a closer look, codependency is about more than just wanting the best for others. Wanting the best for others is usually great. As parents, we pretty much always want the best for our kids, and understandably so! Codependency is not about wanting the best, it's about NEEDING others to be a certain way: _____(fill in the blank). Happy, OK, fulfilled, satisfied, successful, social, and the like. We can't handle it when our children are not being *what we think to be* their best. When we are in our codependency, we experience others' feelings as our own. So, parenting from a codependent place goes well beyond wanting the best for our children. It unconsciously pushes us to try to get them to do what *we think* is best for them, which actually isn't selfless at all. Sometimes, it's even about trying to get them to feel what we think they should. For example, "Johnny should be happy about me setting up a playdate for him." It can also push us not to create or uphold necessary boundaries with our children for fear of how they may react to the boundary; if they feel sad about the boundary, we will feel that sadness as our own, so we don't uphold the boundary, thus not giving them the direction and limits they need from us.

In codependent enmeshment, we feel others' emotions. We tell ourselves we're just trying to make things better or make the other person OK, but we're really just trying to get rid of the feelings we have about what another person is going through. I've worked for years with parents of substance abusers who were stuck in this cycle with their children, trying to control every action, bad decision, or consequence. Doing this only led them to feel depressed, hurt, angry, and out of control. The truth is you can never *control* another person. Some of my most rewarding work has been seeing these parents make changes in their relationships with their children so they don't have to be on the emotional roller coaster anymore.

So, while I believe that codependency can look nice on the surface, it is ultimately a selfish behavior that is destructive to relationships. Codependents are trying to control others so *they* can feel better. They need people to be, feel, and behave a certain way to calm their own anxieties, insecurities, and pain. At the root of this is selfishness; it's all about trying to soothe oneself, just as one does with addiction.

At its worst, codependency makes us lose sight of ourselves. It is not as kind as people see it to be, because beyond trying to control others, we also may ultimately be sacrificing ourselves for someone else, putting excessive amounts of attention on them, and then resenting them for it. I had one parent recently say to me, "When my son was born, everything about me went out the window. My friends and hobbies, especially. It became all about him." EEK! This is codependency at its finest. It's caretaking and putting one's needs *above* your own. Yes, when we first have children, our lives shift dramatically, and we no longer have the same time to dedicate to activities and people we love. However, letting go of all these outlets altogether is highly problematic. What do you think this man is teaching his child? That his son is more important than he is, and that the father should simply let go of himself because he loves his son more than he loves himself. This father proudly knows that his son is aware of his care for him. But what this father is not aware of is that the son internalized how much the father has put onto him and feels overwhelmed by it. Not surprisingly, this child eventually moved far away from his family, most likely due to his complicated feelings over his father being too focused on him at all times and the resulting pressure of that. Codependent love can push our children away because it is smothering and controlling. A healthier approach is to find the balance between loving our children and loving ourselves. Letting them grow and be independent versus trying to micromanage their every move.

My husband and I have worked on this a lot since having two children. We're not perfect with it, but we've made an agreement to set aside time for the important parts of our individual lives outside the family. We want our children to see us take care of ourselves and enjoy our independent interests and passions. My husband plays in a basketball league once a week to maintain his physical activity and love of basketball. And I make time to attend a women's group once a month and go to yoga weekly. We also make time to do fun things as a couple, like going out to dinner or spending time with our friends.

In our society we tend to praise people who are codependent as "so nice, kind, or loving." We don't often consider how their behavior is manipulative and negative to relationships. We don't realize that these same people are also silently feeling negative feelings as a result of putting others first, resenting others for "taking so much." For example, consider a wife and mother who "does it all," never asking her husband for help because she feels responsible for keeping the house tidy and the kids fed, and managing everyone's well-being. She creates stories about what would happen if she didn't do it, like *It wouldn't get done* or *He'll be angry if I ask him for help.* She says everything is fine, yet she withholds sex from her husband because she's "not interested," when really she's angry about giving too much. Resentment will slowly chip away at this type of relationship, often ending in some large fight over the many unspoken issues lingering within the codependent dynamic.

Or in the previous case of the codependent father, what happens further down the line when his son becomes an adult?

What has he learned about being an independent person outside of the relationship with his father? What has he learned about what it means to be a parent? Unless he works to break the cycle, he will pass the codependent dynamic on to his own children. To prevent this as parents, we need to let our children step up into their own lives, hold them accountable for taking care of themselves, and show them what it looks like to take care of ourselves separately from them.

My own codependency has taken several forms. One was not speaking up when I needed to. Another was saying yes when I meant no. When someone else was disappointed, I tried (frantically at times) to make sure they were OK. I would go to engagements I didn't want to attend. I would tell people what they wanted to hear, instead of what they may have needed to hear, just so I didn't hurt their feelings. I would let other people make plans for me, because I "didn't care what we did." (Or at least that's what I told them.)

I felt as if I didn't have any control in my relationships. Then I'd resent the other people, as if they were somehow doing something to me. I put all my focus on other people instead of on myself. In a talk he had with Oprah about this exact issue, Dr. Phil used a wonderful analogy of having the key to start a car. He said when you believe the other person has your key, you will stay stuck, waiting forever for them to give you your key. But the truth is that it's you and only you who holds the keys to your own life. You are the only one who has the ability to change your relationships with others. You can't sit around waiting for them to change. This is what we will continue to explore in this book, especially in regards to parenting.

For me, codependency was powerlessness. It was feeling obligated to others. It was trying to manipulate people's feelings so they could feel the way I wanted them to feel. Unfortunately, all of my many forms of codependent behavior built up lots of anger that would come out at inopportune times or among the wrong people. Thankfully, as I've learned to release the anger in appropriate ways and with the right people and at the right times, I no longer live in a place of holding onto that anger in a destructive way. Needless to say, I had a lot of fear about having children because of my tendency for codependency and putting others' needs above my own. I even made a promise to myself that I wouldn't have children until I felt my codependency was in remission enough that I wouldn't be swallowed alive by my children and their needs.

The ironic thing about codependency is that you work so hard but never really make anyone happy, definitely not yourself. It can lead us to be dishonest and passive-aggressive and STILL not get what we want, instead of simply saying what we mean and meaning what we say.

When we are in our codependency with our children, we leave them confused. Our words aren't in alignment with our behavior or actions. We say we're not mad when it's clear we are. Our children always know the truth. And when we try to hide or lie about how we feel, our children learn not to trust us. They also don't learn how to express themselves honestly or deal with relationship difficulties effectively. When we don't know how to say no, we teach them to do things they don't want to do so as not to upset others. For example, a friend of mine was encouraging her child to give people hugs even when the child didn't want to. She asked me what I thought about this, and I shared that I felt it encouraged her child not to say no when she needed to. As parents, we should want our children to be able to say no when they don't want people touching them. It's important for them to create physical boundaries with others. By encouraging her child to "be polite" and give hugs even when she didn't want to, this mother was teaching her child to ignore her own boundaries.

Another issue with codependency is that it prevents us from really connecting to others. I believe that my codependency was making me sick physically, energetically, and spiritually. It was creating great stress in my life and in my body. I was drained of energy for many years. I was resenting many people in my life, believing it was they who were causing me distress while I was waiting for them to change so I could feel better. I wasn't really living for me; I was living someone else's life, never reaching for my highest potential. Working through my codependency was tough. With the aid of my therapist, I began going through every relationship in my life to see where I wasn't being true to myself and was giving too much to others. I looked at my daily experiences and explored where I may have said yes when I meant no. I processed the past and where I had taken wrong turns away from myself to please someone else. I had to find myself, which meant taking time to make thoughtful decisions about how I wanted to be who I wanted to be, how I wanted to feel. I needed to both step up and let go at the same time.

SELF-LOVE

In healing codependency, we need to consider the balance between selfish and selfless behavior. Many people are concerned that being less selfless will lead them to become selfish. At times, this may be the case. Often before we find balance, we go to the other extreme. But there *is* a healthy medium between selfless and selfish, and I call that place self-love. This is what we need to strive for.

As I healed from codependency, I began to find my SELF. I began to feel my own needs and identify them. I learned to speak up and express myself in a way that wasn't about being harsh, mean, or nasty, but was about saying what was true for me. I began living in self-love, learning how to take care of myself and be nurturing and loving to myself as well as to others! I no longer had to suppress all my feelings; I began to slowly let them out in a way that felt honest. I began to communicate clearly. I stopped trying to make other people be who and what I thought I needed them to be. I began to let go of expectations that people should act, live, or feel a certain way. I learned to let people in who could support me and allowed myself to ask for and receive what I needed from them.

Going through this process wasn't easy then and remains difficult now. It took a lot of hard work and some really difficult experiences and conversations. Some relationships ended, despite my not wanting them to end. But I tried and kept at it. I will talk later in the book about how my codependency has manifested as a parent. As a recovering codependent, a lot comes up for me with parenting, and the experience pushes me to further my own recovery in whole new ways. In the next section of the book, we'll explore the link between codependency and parenting specifically.

CHAPTER 2

PERFECTIONISM

Perfectionism, in simple terms, means holding ourselves to unrealistic standards that we will never attain. When we have these lofty expectations for ourselves, we are likely to put them on others, especially our children. This can be very difficult and sad for a child. Perfectionists are tough: tough on themselves and tough on those around them. They use indicators of achievement to determine their self-worth. They are always striving to meet their next goal in order to feel better—because *just being* is not enough.

Perfectionist parenting, according to Brené Brown in *Daring Greatly*, is "teaching [our children] to value what other people think over what they think or how they feel. It's teaching them to perform, please, and prove." Many of us who are perfectionist parents grew up as little perfectionists. We were pushed to excel in school, go to a great college, and be stellar athletes or performers. We may have even been encouraged to lose weight or maintain a particular appearance. Perfectionists can be very competitive people. Your parents may have been excessively critical of you or overlooked your mental health in favor of checking off external indicators of success. It's tough to learn to accept ourselves as we are when the messages we receive tell us not to.

When I was a child, perfectionism manifested itself in several ways. I avoided doing things I knew I wouldn't do well, which meant I was too scared to try new creative endeavors, and I resisted putting myself out there for fear that I wouldn't be "the best." I had so little confidence in many parts of myself that I was preventing myself from being vulnerable. Sadly, this meant that I avoided trying many things I may have really enjoyed throughout my life. I definitely do not want to pass this trait on to my own children. I want them to explore all that life has to offer. I don't want them to only try things so they can be the best at them, but so they can genuinely have fun and feel the joy that comes with learning and growing and being outside our comfort zones.

Not surprisingly, growing up I always had an intense need for straight As. I was good at school and got positive feedback for those achievements, so I held onto that affirmation and strived for it constantly. My need for success created tremendous stress—to the extent that my hair started falling out when I was in high school! My life was all about achieving, and this continued throughout college and graduate school. (It didn't help that my college gave a $10,000 scholarship for students who maintained a GPA above 3.75. Of course I had to achieve this!) This was all part of my perfectionism until I realized it was making me sick. I would get sick with bronchitis or pneumonia once a semester from all the stress I was putting on myself. I wasn't enjoying the journey or process of learning. The only goals were to get good grades and to win. It still saddens me to think about all I missed out on because of this laser focus.

Perfectionism develops as a way to please our parents, teachers, and other people in our lives. To try to be better than others so we can feel superior. It's about "being good" so we can be loved, appreciated, and admired. Perfectionists are scared of failure, judgment, disapproval, and ridicule, so we perform in order to protect ourselves against those negative experiences. In adulthood, my perfectionism manifested as a desire for people to see me as flawless. I tried to give myself a (false) sense of security by *making sure* I was doing nothing other people could judge me for (an impossible objective, let me assure you). This only led to more striving.

It's important to note that not all perfectionists are strivers. Some give up early on because they feel they will always fall short of the expectations placed upon them—they don't even try. They pull themselves out of the game so they can have control over it. Many of my clients in recovery from substance abuse fall under this type of perfectionist. This is especially common in wealthy or successful families, where expectations can feel extremely overwhelming. Recovering addicts often don't realize they are also perfectionists until they get clean and begin to see things clearly. Many of the parents I work with whose children have substance abuse issues think that their children simply don't care. But it's quite the opposite. They actually care *too much*, and it becomes overwhelming and eventually debilitating for them.

Perfectionism can cause us to hide our shortcomings, pain, and struggles. We don't want people to judge us, so we never share what we're really going through, instead painting a perfect picture. This leads us far away from our true selves, and it isn't good for other people either. It keeps people at arm's length and may also make them feel bad about themselves if they have struggles in their own lives. It prevents a real connection with others. Perfectionism also stunts creativity. It doesn't allow us to explore, try new things, or be human. Instead, it rigidly defines what life is "supposed" to look like. It takes away from the fun and growth that come from exploration and adventure. When things like grades, accolades, or promotions define who we are, how smart we are, and how much we're worth, we remain locked in our comfort zone. As parents, we need to help our children move away from using such arbitrary standards to measure who they are. Home should be a safe space to not have to be perfect—to be accepted for exactly who we are.

PERFECTIONISM AND PARENTING

I remember a time when my perfectionism came out in full force—it embarrasses me to think about it now. I was at a family friend's home with their young child, who had just had some pasta with marinara sauce. The sauce was all over her face. I was pregnant and remember my body recoiling from the child looking so messy. *How could they let her look like that with a guest here?* my perfectionist brain judged. *How terrible.* Now as a parent, I see how ridiculous that was, but my perfectionist nonparent looked at those parents with disdain. I needed a big reality check, and I got it as soon as I had my own toddler running around the house—with food on her face. Looking back at this moment, I can see that it wasn't really me speaking, but my perfectionism. My judgment of others back then stemmed from the deep judgment I had for myself.

Perfectionism is ingrained in me at a deep level, and I still struggle to separate from it. It will always be part of my journey as a parent! I catch myself wanting my daughters to wear certain outfits or do their hair in the ways I think look best. In these moments, I have to stop and remind myself that it's my perfectionism talking and instead let my kids be who they are.

> Remi, a forty-one-year-old woman, came to see me for supervision of her work as a life coach. After some brief work with Remi, it became clear that she had a lot of perfectionist tendencies. Remi came from a religious household with two parents who she described as loving and caring. Remi also reported having issues with her body image, thinking she was overweight and constantly beating herself up over being less than perfect. In our work, it came out that Remi had an eating disorder (a common issue with perfectionist people). After we built up some trust within our therapeutic work, Remi revealed that her parents were hyperfocused on her weight growing up. They couldn't stand her being "overweight" and constantly told her that she needed to be mindful of what she ate. Remi even recalled a moment where her parents were arguing about how fat she was (when they thought she couldn't hear them) and whose fault it was that she was overweight. From the looks of Remi, most people would not consider her weight to be an issue, but perfectionists just can't accept less than perfect. Remi's parents repeatedly told her that they were helping her lose weight for her "own good" so "other people didn't make fun" of her, when in reality *they* were the ones damaging her self-esteem.
>
> Through our work together, Remi began to realize that her perception of herself as fat was really distorted. She realized she was seeing herself through the lens of her parents rather than her own reality. After much therapeutic work, Remi was able to begin to be

> more loving toward herself. She quit dieting and began working on acceptance instead.

Although Remi's parents may have really thought they were being helpful in trying to get their daughter to look a certain way, it's clear they were anything but helpful. It's important to reflect on your own perfectionist tendencies and then examine how they may show up in your parenting.

AM I A PERFECTIONIST?

- Do you feel you need to look a particular way that society deems beautiful?

- Are you preoccupied with weight loss or managing a particular weight? Do you diet often?

- Do you have trouble leaving the house without putting yourself together (e.g., wearing makeup, ironed clothes, etc.)?

- Do you use your job to define your worth?

- Are you constantly striving for more—money, promotions, accomplishments?

- Do you often compare yourself to others?

- Do you feel like you never accomplish enough in a day?

- Do you clean your house excessively before people come over?

- Do you resist trying new activities because you might not be good at them?

- Do you have trouble seeing yourself as creative?

- Do you have judgments about people you consider less than perfect due to appearance, weight, or socioeconomic status?

- Do you beat yourself up for failures? Even minor ones, such as being awkward in a conversation or not saying the right thing?

- Do you tend to be more focused on what you haven't accomplished than on what you have?

- Do you have trouble allowing yourself downtime or time just to relax?

- Do you have trouble taking time off of work to simply enjoy yourself when it's not part of a vacation or other planned occasion?

- Do you have trouble being compassionate with yourself?

- Do you have trouble celebrating your accomplishments?

- Do you tend to spend excessive time on activities in order to be the best at them?

- Do you have trouble acknowledging yourself as being good at something if you aren't where you ultimately want to be with it?

- Do you push those around you to "be their best" even when it doesn't seem to be something they are interested in?

- Do you have a voice in your head that often puts you down, telling you you're not worthy, smart enough, good enough, etc.?

- Do you find yourself procrastinating often?

- Do you have trouble taking in constructive criticism?

- When you receive perceived negative feedback, can it feel disabling at times?

- Do you find yourself acting, dressing, or speaking in a way to ensure you don't look "stupid" or "silly" to others?

If you answered yes to one or two of these questions, you may have some slight perfectionist tendencies. If you answered yes to between three and five questions, you can consider yourself a perfectionist. If you answered yes to more than five questions, you are a serious perfectionist. It will be helpful to examine the root of your perfectionism and work to separate it from your parenting style.

HEALING PERFECTIONIST HABITS

If we can let go of the perfectionist mindset, we can let go of our superficial needs in order to be present and loving parents *to the people our children are*. This will also stop us from creating more miniature perfectionists. The first step in avoiding perfectionist parenting is to heal your own perfectionist tendencies. I now know that I'm not perfect in my body, my behavior, my work, my parenting, or any other aspect of my life—and I never will be. I try to honor and love myself for my whole self, including my shortcomings and missteps. Having daughters, I feel it's especially important to model that I love and accept myself. I know they will be more likely to accept themselves if they see me doing it. I also joke often about the mistakes I make rather than getting frustrated or obsessing. I want them to see what it looks like to keep things light and have fun . . . and let things go. I also apologize and acknowledge when I've done something that may have harmed or hurt someone else. I've learned to let go of needing particular outcomes or of needing things to look a particular way. I work on it every day.

Because we inhabit a world in which we have little control over outcomes, our human lives require a tremendous amount of faith. And I will say, nothing makes me feel more out of control than being a parent. There's *so* little we can control when it comes to our kids! Just spend a few hours with a toddler or a teenager and you'll know what I mean. I've created this guide to help you release control, become more present and loving in your parenting, and enjoy it—all for the betterment of your children and especially for yourself. Releasing control means doing what you can to the best of your abilities and letting go of the rest, trusting you've done enough. It is about listening to your gut, or inner knowing. Ultimately, it's knowing that the Universe has control in the end, not you or me or anyone else. From this state of mind, it becomes easier to trust that our children are also exactly who and where they need to be—and that we don't need to control everything they do, achieve, or become.

The first step to healing perfectionism is putting less focus on your and your children's external accomplishments. My goal here is to help you move away from focusing on your child's achievements and toward focusing on *who they are as soulful beings*. The goal is for you to help your children cope with feelings, learn how to reground and soothe themselves, and work through any hardships or traumas they may experience. These abilities will set them up to become balanced, functional adults far more than any external achievement or A+ grade will. As Brené Brown explains in *Daring Greatly*, "We numb the pain that comes from feeling inadequate and 'less than'. . . . The most powerful need for numbing seems to come from a combination of . . . shame, anxiety, and disconnection." We want to avoid sending our children down this path of numbing, shame, and avoidance. As parents, we want to create an environment that makes space for and honors their full human experience, regardless of external factors. This is where real resiliency and authenticity are born.

THE CODEPENDENT PERFECTIONIST

If you're having trouble sitting with the idea of being a codependent or a perfectionist—or both, like me—you're not alone. It's tough to acknowledge this stuff, so be sure to have some compassion for yourself. In my journey, I had a lot of larger codependency issues I needed to face before I could even look at my perfectionism, because it was affecting me much more strongly, and I knew it would be a major issue in my future parenting. But as I peeled back the layers of codependency, the power of perfectionism began to emerge. And I've identified this same combination in many of my clients.

We've examined how our society is reinforcing for codependents. By this, I mean how we're often taught from an early age not to feel certain feelings and also to feel responsible for managing other people's lives and experiences. Our society is also very much geared toward perfectionist behavior. Where I live, in New York City, I see this everywhere. We are driven relentlessly to succeed in our careers, work at all hours, not put up boundaries with our employers, and wear busyness as a badge of honor while still projecting the image of a perfect life. In our society, we like to place people in boxes based on their achievements, and we *don't* like to acknowledge the gray area where we all actually live—the place where we all have human flaws, make missteps, and exist in less-than-perfect relationships, including our parent/child relationship.

Codependents tend to have issues with perfectionism and vice versa. Shame and feelings of worthlessness or not being good enough are at the core of both of these issues. We don't feel lovable just being who we really are, and so we go to codependency and perfectionism to seek love and acceptance from others. For parents, this issue is so pervasive because (when these issues aren't healed) our children are unconsciously seen as an extension of ourselves. When we feel a sense of shame about who we are, we unknowingly pass this on to our children, instinctively looking for them to change our experience of ourselves that we project onto them. This can be difficult to understand, but it's important to really look at what your children bring up for you.

Having both codependent and perfectionist issues leads to unique challenges. Let's take a look at Johana below.

Johana and her husband, Bradley, have a five-year-old daughter, Simone. Simone was a quiet child who was seen as easygoing. Johana, having not worked on her codependency and perfectionism, didn't realize that she was pushing her young child to be different from who she was, leaving her feeling not accepted. She would have her take part in sports she wasn't interested in, while standing on the sidelines yelling for her daughter to participate and "score a goal!" She put her into dance, gymnastics, swimming, and all sorts of extracurricular activities to get her to flourish in something. But Simone simply wasn't interested. She loved reading and playing alone, creating magical stories and acting them out. Johana was also pushing her child to speak up and stand up for herself, but Simone simply didn't have that type of personality; she was more of an introvert. She rejected her mother pushing her and became even more reserved.

Johana came to see me after an experience where some children at school had told Simone she couldn't play with them on the playground. Johana lost it and had an outburst at Simone's teacher for "not protecting her from these other children!" "How dare they say that to my child and for no one to have stepped in!" The teacher tried to explain to Johana that these experiences are normal and that she did speak with all the children and let them know this was unacceptable. But for Johana this wasn't enough.

Johana was unaware that everything that was going on with her child was bringing up difficult feelings from her own childhood. Johana was a codependent perfectionist. She always wanted to be accepted and seen as a winner, so she worked hard to cultivate a persona that included her being great at everything she put her mind

> to. She was outgoing, smart, and popular. She believed it was her job to make sure her daughter had these same qualities, caring as much about how other people saw her. She was enmeshed with her child in every way. Johana couldn't simply accept her daughter as being anything less than what she expected of her.

Codependent perfectionists have a lot of trouble accepting things as they are and *just being*, which makes us discontent in the present moment. Our sense of security tends to come from external events—other people's behavior (codependency) or our own achievements (perfectionism)—rather than internal well-being. And so we are constantly focused on things outside of ourselves that we believe will make us feel good or provide us with the perception that we are finally in control.

It's important to note that not all codependents are perfectionists, and vice versa. And we are not all these things to the same degree—and our tendencies can shift throughout our lives. While reading this book, you may find yourself identifying more strongly with one over the other. Either way, use what relates to you and let the rest go. As you begin to become more aware of these tendencies, you may see different aspects emerge from those you may have expected. That's great because it means you're starting to see things as they really are.

One way to spot your own codependent perfectionist tendencies is by looking at how often you utilize if/when-then statements. I do this exercise with my clients. Try filling in the blanks for your present state of mind.

IF/WHEN _____ HAPPENS,
THEN I WILL FEEL _____ .

Examples I hear in my practice include:

- When I can finally afford to buy my first home, then I'll feel happy.
- When my son stops using opiates, I'll be OK.
- When I get a raise, then I'll feel good.
- When my husband does what I want, we'll have a better marriage.

We use these experiences to tell ourselves that external events will change our reality and make us feel good. This is, sadly, a false hope—and one we can waste our lives chasing.

What we want to show our children instead is how to be content in life regardless of what's going on around us. When we unravel our codependent and perfectionist tendencies, we can finally provide this example for our kids. It's important that your children don't believe that they need something or someone to feel good. Help your children be present with themselves, with their lives, and with their emotional experiences. Help them move from finding security in what's going on outside of them to what's going on inside of them. When we do this, accomplishments, success, and the relationships we have become the icing on the cake, rather than the key ingredients for our mental wellness.

CHAPTER 3

YOU DON'T OWN YOUR CHILDREN

I want my children to feel heard, seen, and accepted. I want them to feel encouraged and empowered. As a parent, I want to be present and loving. It is important to me to discourage codependency and perfectionism, even though both traits are promoted by society as we experience increasing pressure to conform and achieve. This is my vision as a parent. Your vision may be similar or different, but either way, having a vision can help you work toward the kind of parenting you believe in. It also provides you with a compass when you're lost and confused.

My vision for parenting also includes the idea that we do not own our children, that they are not *ours*, as possessions are ours. There's a wonderful Native American saying that goes, *Remember that your children are not your own but are lent to you by the Creator.* I remind myself of this mantra often; it helps me let go and allow my children to evolve in their own beautiful ways.

Ownership is, in fact, a large part of the issue of codependency. Being codependent carries with it the idea that we are responsible for controlling our children's behavior, which can lead to a more authoritarian parenting style. We don't want to control our children in this way. If we do this, we are likely to have children who either acquiesce to us or rebel against us. In the case of the child who acquiesces, they are likely to become codependent, unable to speak up for and assert themselves throughout their life.

I remember a family member of mine once mentioning being embarrassed over another family member's behavior. I thought to myself, "How can you be embarrassed if it wasn't you who acted that way?" As I grew older and came into my more codependent ways, I realized that many of us have an underlying belief that just because someone is our spouse, sister, father, or child, we are somehow responsible for what they do and say. We believe we have the right to tell them that their behavior, thoughts, or attitudes are not acceptable because on some level, we believe these people are a reflection of us.

Does any of this sound familiar?

TREAT FAMILY AS FRIENDS

One way to work out of this pattern is to begin treating our family as friends. Think about it: Most of us treat our friendships *very* differently from our family relationships. Usually in a friendship, we don't have an illusion of ownership over the other person. We often aren't as codependent. We tend to be more supportive and less controlling, and we don't feel the need to tell our friends how they should act, feel, look, talk, or behave. It's amazing how transformative relationships can be when we let go of needing the other person to be a certain way. Sometimes, I tell my clients to imagine that they are dealing with a friend rather than a family member. I ask them how that would change their reaction to the situation. It's a pretty illuminating exercise.

This concept also applies to parenting. It's not exactly the same, of course, because we are responsible for our children and their general well-being when they are minors. And it's especially difficult to implement when our kids are young. But just as in friendships, we want to come at parenting from a place of both connection and separation. We want to see our children not as extensions of ourselves, but as unique beings whom we can help guide on their journey. We want to be mindful not to assert control over them and direct them to be and act as we would want, and to take into consideration at all times who they are, giving them support without interfering with their necessary growth.

Parents need to be careful about trying to direct the course of a child's life. This applies to the day-to-day as well as the bigger picture. Consider for a moment how often you tell your child not to do something. Or how often you make a decision for them because you feel it's "in their best interest." Just as you do with your friends, give your child space to make decisions, handle situations in the way they think is best, and fail when they need to. Speak to them as you would a friend, from a place of concern when needed, not a place of authority or thinking you "know better."

This is especially important with teenagers. We don't want to actually be their friends (and they don't want this either), but rather to find the balance of being their parent and letting go. If we've done the work early on to connect with them from this place of healthy separation, we are likely to have an easier time in their teen years because they will know they have enough space to grow without feeling disconnected from us. When we have parented without codependency and perfectionism, they will also be able to trust that we *really* have their best interests in mind and are not simply trying to control them. Language is very important in how we guide them during this time. Some people say things to their children that they would never say to their friends, such as *You're being lazy* or *You shouldn't eat that*. The reality is, if we treated our friends how we treat our children, we probably wouldn't have a lot of friends.

It's also important to look at the obligations you unknowingly impose upon your children simply because they are *your* children. This makes me think of a mother I worked with who was very upset with her adult son. Her son was equally as upset with his mother. The mother would endlessly say to me, "But, Alana, he's my son, he should ____. And after all I've done for him!" This encompassed everything from asking how her day was, to calling her more often, to helping out with the care of her dogs, to spending a certain amount of time with her. I worked with this mother on having a more friendship-like relationship with her son, loosening her unrealistic expectations of him. This made a huge shift in the relationship because it took away a lot of unnecessary strings that were attached and creating resentments between the mother and son.

Give to your children without strings attached. Only do what feels right and not what you think will come back to you if you do it. Do the same with friends. Lessen your expectations of what you believe your children owe you for what you've done for them. You choose to have children—they don't owe you anything except respect. And always keep in mind that children come into this world on their own journey. They have many things to learn and experience in this lifetime. If we can do our best at not feeling like we own them, we give them a better shot at successfully navigating what it is they're here to work on. We also have a better shot at truly connecting with our children when they feel that we are just here to love them fully.

BE A LEADER AND A GUIDE

Because I don't believe that I own my children, I also don't operate according to the idea that it is my job to continuously tell them how to be and what to do. When I share this point of view with clients, they often look at me confused. One client who had an especially overbearing father even told me that his father called my ideas "some ridiculous, New Age shit." Ha! But being a leader or guide for our children does not mean that we take a hands-off approach. When you are a good guide, you are totally in tune with those you are leading—you know what they need, their strengths and weaknesses, and how to draw out the best in them. Presence is key. If you are directing someone else as if you own them, you are likely *less* aware of their needs in the moment. This approach doesn't mean I don't express my own thoughts or beliefs to my children. I often intervene, especially if I feel that my children are being unkind to one another or doing something that jeopardizes their safety or the safety of others. However, I am careful with my words, attitude, and energy. I am careful not to intervene from a place of control.

As leaders of our families, we have to lead by example. We want to model balance and make decisions from our best self. This means we actually have to live how we parent—not just tell our children what to do. Imagine for a moment (and yes, I do this with clients often) that you can't give anyone in your life advice on anything you're not doing for yourself. Pretty profound, right? We should all have to live what we teach; we have to show our children, not just tell them. That's what conscious or aware parenting looks like. More on this later.

I take this same approach as a boss and supervisor. Instead of focusing on what I don't want my employees or colleagues to do, I focus on who I want them to become. This is less about behavior management and more about fostering their growth. Along with my business partner, we set up an entire business model to help other therapists begin their own private practices and grow into the wellness professional of their dreams. I do this by encouraging them, supporting them, and teaching them how to be on their own. When we want people to grow, we don't want to shame them; we want to provide support, build them up, and help them heal. As a boss or leader, sometimes I need to make many difficult decisions—just like with parenting. (The main difference being that I may have to let someone go if it's not working out in my business, and that sure doesn't fly with my kids . . . although there have been times when I've wanted to say, *You're fired!*)

Many parents don't realize that they're subconsciously operating as if they have ownership of their children. I want to dispute the idea that, as parents, we are our children's "keepers." This is tough, since we do so much to care for our children and are entrusted with their survival from the day of their birth. However, when we have that sense of ownership, what often follows is a parents-know-best approach. In my work, I've found this approach is most often rooted in fear.

As parents, we often make decisions out of fear—fear of the unknown, of looking deeper into what will happen to our children and how we will feel about it. We may believe it's our job to somehow know what our children need, more than our child or the Universe does, and feel we must teach them, sometimes through coercive means, that we are right at all times. Sometimes we even do this through emotionally manipulative means. We may not even realize this because we assume we're just "doing what's best for them" or "making sure they don't get hurt." But that mentality goes along with the belief that our children should do things our way. How do we know if our way is actually best for *them*? We don't. And that's why this approach tends to set up a negative power dynamic with children.

RAISE EMPOWERED CHILDREN

When I bring up power dynamics, people tend to raise an eyebrow and assume I'm trying to tell them that their child should be in charge. But understanding power is important. As parents, ultimately, we are (or need to be) the authority in the relationship with our children, and they do need to know this. However, if our children feel *dis*empowered, we are most likely doing them a great disservice and creating a situation in which they don't feel heard, seen, or accepted. Parents usually use power to make them feel this way. You may ask, *How can we be an authority and have our children feel empowered at the same time?* It's possible! But it's a delicate balance.

It may help to think about work again. Have you ever had a boss who felt like a dictator? It's likely you felt disempowered in this situation, having no voice and just feeling like their minion. Now think of a boss who didn't make you feel this way. The most effective bosses are still authority figures yet are open and interested in what their employees think, feel, and experience in the workplace. They still have the final say on important decisions, but they create a safe space so that you feel included. You feel heard and seen. You feel respected.

You want to create a similar dynamic in your home so your children feel heard, seen, and respected. This book will teach you how to do that. You also want them to feel like they can make decisions for themselves. Not all decisions or every decision, but a good portion of decisions. Avoid making all decisions for them, which can start at an early age: what they wear, how they want their hair to look, and maybe what activities they want to participate in. One way to foster decision-making skills with boundaries is to give them several options you're comfortable with and allow them to choose which one they want, for instance what to have for breakfast or a snack.

I speak more about power later in the book, but if there's anything I want you to take away, it's to try not to assert power over your children in a tyrannical way. Tyrannical parenting leaves our children feeling unloved. This is foundational to codependency and perfectionism issues, as well as a range of other mental health issues. What we really need to learn is who our children are in order to make the best decisions for them and, more importantly, to help them make the best decisions for themselves. If we operate out of strict adherence to rules, or what we have always thought of as being *right*, we will probably squelch our children's growth, which can lead to all sorts of behavioral issues throughout their lives.

WE ARE OUR OWN EXPERTS

One of the premises I utilize in my work with my clients is that they are their own experts. This informs how I assist them in their healing process. This means that I believe my clients actually have all their own answers. On a deep and often unconscious level, they know who they are and what they need. Our true self resides within our soul. It is simply my job to guide clients there.

Because of this, I believe in "holding space" for my clients in a way that allows them to find these answers within. I also believe this applies to parenting. Now, this doesn't mean I don't give my clients advice at times, especially when they ask for it. But I am very careful not to impose myself or dictate what they should do or how they should feel. I also practice this with my children. If you are the expert of yourself, then it only makes sense that your children are their own experts as well.

When we act as guides for our children, we learn to resist telling them what they should be doing (as hard as this may be) and begin to recognize that we don't have all their answers. We start to believe that they are their own experts. Let's take a look at a wonderful and caring parent with whom I have worked for many years. She has a big heart and cares deeply for her children. She fought for them for many years from a loving place. However, she's also struggled with her codependency, which impacts her ability to let go and let her children learn the hard lessons they need to learn in order to thrive.

> Janelle is a middle-aged woman with teenage daughters. One is a high achiever, and the other has been in and out of treatment programs since she was a young teen. Suzanne is struggling to complete high school, showing little motivation to obtain her diploma. She has been struggling with anxiety and depression since the age of twelve. While she's worked on her mental health, and her problems have been in remission for months at a time, she still shows little motivation in life.
>
> Suzanne wasn't in crisis when Janelle came to see me, but she was at a loss for what to do. She said, "Alana, I don't want Suzanne to throw her life away." Janelle felt it was her job to frantically give Suzanne suggestions and to make sure she got her diploma and went on to college so she could become successful.
>
> I agreed with Janelle that something needed to be done. However, I pointed out that making every conversation a "teaching moment" had caused Suzanne to stop telling Janelle what was truly going on with her. She felt she couldn't share, because every time she did,

she received a lecture on what she should do, which only led to more anxiety and depression. They were clearly disconnected.

Janelle felt her way was right and could not imagine dealing with Suzanne any differently. (Despite the fact that it wasn't working!) Of course, Janelle and her husband were coming from a place of care and concern, but they had trouble seeing that it was actually *not* loving to force their views, beliefs, and ideas onto another person. What they actually needed to learn was how to back off. That didn't mean to stop loving or caring for Suzanne. In fact, it meant becoming more loving.

After years of forcing her into treatment and using various measures to get her to recover and graduate from high school, they had created a power struggle in Suzanne's life rather than fostering a natural desire for their daughter to reclaim her life and make it what she wanted.

Meanwhile, Suzanne's sister, Sheila, was the high-achieving child. However, Sheila had a lot of anger that she couldn't cope with. She felt resentful of all the energy, time, and space that Suzanne had taken up in the family because of her parents' codependent and perfectionist obsession on Suzanne. This family needed a big shift in the way they were attending to their daughters. They needed to stop focusing so heavily on school achievement as an indicator of how their kids were doing and trying to force them to do well, and learn how to reconnect with them not from a place of codependency or perfectionism but simply love.

FOCUS ON THE INTERNAL, NOT THE EXTERNAL

Because my parenting vision is mostly about guiding my children to grow into loving beings who feel empowered to go out and take on the world, I know that my focus needs to be on their internal emotional growth rather than on external signifiers of "success." When we focus on building up someone internally, we help them build a strong foundation that can help them in all aspects of life. As the saying goes, *Give a man a fish, feed him for day; teach a man to fish, feed him for a lifetime.* We want to feed our children for a lifetime! Focusing on getting As in school, rather than gaining knowledge, insisting they be the best on their sports team, rather than having fun and building team skills, or making sure they are well put together, rather than confident in themselves, are all external goals. They are more about perfectionism and codependency than anything else.

When we focus on these facets of life, we tend to take our children away from their true selves and closer to societal expectations. Our society tends to view success in external measures: Where did they go to college? Is he married? Does she have a good job? Have they bought a house? Sadly, we so often don't look at the real person but only life markers to judge well-being. What this leads to is many empty people trying to attain external goals that they believe will make them happy (and this is perfectionism). With our children, it's not about what you do, but who you are. Are you true to yourself? Are you living with passion and purpose? Do you feel your life has meaning? Do you feel excited about the life you're living? Do you live with a sense of integrity? These are the things that are truly important.

To go back to Janelle for a moment, she later told me that one of the most impactful statements I made to her was when I told her she doesn't know why Suzanne is meant to go through the struggles she has and where it may bring her. Sometimes, battling a mental health issue in one's life may be exactly what one needs to do to become an expert in the field, maybe eventually helping others in crisis. When we can see our child's experiences this way, we are living in trust. We allow them to go through the difficulties on their own path while trying to build them up internally and also creating boundaries to minimize the potential for negative outcomes. If you look at your own life, can you see all the times you went through something difficult just to come out on the other end with a greater understanding of yourself? Can you understand how focusing on the internal versus the external may be more impactful for our children in the long run?

REFLECTIVE EXERCISE

Please take this time to sit quietly and focus on your breath, relaxing your muscles from your head down to your feet. It may be helpful to breathe in for a count of four and then out for a count of four. Envision your ideal outcome in parenting. What do your children embody in this vision? Are they curious? Competent? Self-sufficient? Emotionally stable? Do they feel confident with being who they really are? Do they take reasonable risks? Do they use drugs, alcohol, food, or another mechanism to soothe their discomfort? How close do you feel to them? Can they trust you? Do they open up to you to explore their struggles? Do they feel respected, heard, and seen?

Notice if your vision of parenting includes external factors (e.g., *I see them as a lawyer, graduating college, having a beautiful wedding*). If so (and many of us will have these visions—we've been conditioned to think this way!), stop and examine them. Consider what they're really about. See if you can shift the vision to focus on an internal factor instead.

Write, draw, or collage this vision. Refer back to it whenever you feel like you're in the weeds as a parent. It will help you get back to what's important. The rest of this book is meant to help guide you in attaining this vision.

CHAPTER 4

TRANSITIONAL PARENTING

Transitional parenting is an adaptive approach to parenting in which we grow *with* our children. This means we don't hold a rigid idea of who they are or how they should act at any point in time. Instead we adapt to the person growing in front of us. We don't try to force them into some sort of perfectionist box. We don't hover over them as codependents. Instead we witness and honor their journey. If we want them to discover themselves, we must act as observers rather than as intruders.

I once attended a training session with a great neuropsychologist. He discussed raising his children and how his professional expertise had impacted some of his parenting choices. When the training was over, perfectionist me went up to him and asked, "So, what preschool model do you think is best for my children?" He looked at me and said, "I don't know because

I don't know your children!" We laughed at my perfectionist question and then spoke about the importance of finding the right fit for *my* child. He also told me that he sent each of his children to different schools because they had different needs. This really resonated. It's all about knowing *your* children and what they need at any given time. I've been aware from an early age that my daughters' brains take in information and learn differently. I can tell this from how they play, and so I know that they may have very different needs in school or different reactions to the same teaching styles.

A family member of mine once commented that the most problematic parenting comes from those who say, *I don't know what happened. I treated all my kids the same.* She joked, "That's the problem! How could you possibly parent them all the same?" In understanding each child, we recognize that they have unique needs, and therefore our parenting is unique for each of them. I hold this philosophy not just as a parent, but also as a manager at work. Think about all your employees or coworkers and how different their needs are, based on what they bring to the table. As a boss, you can't possibly treat all your employees exactly the same and expect the same outcome. You always need to consider the individual.

Also, as humans, our needs change and evolve over time. What fits our personalities when we're very young children may not anymore when we're in elementary school. Give your children space to grow and change. Some kids start off shy and become gregarious. Don't label your children in a way that limits them. Our children are trying on different qualities and versions of themselves to figure out who they are. This is a lifelong process.

> One of the greatest difficulties my client Janice faced with her parents was their inability to transition with

> her as she evolved. In their minds, she was still their quiet, shy, five-year-old child. But in reality, she had become a successful woman, mother, and wife who was no longer quiet or shy! Instead of treating her like the adult she was, Janice's parents were stuck in the past, still speaking to their daughter as if she weren't confident or capable. This created a great disconnect between them. Janice felt she couldn't have an authentic relationship with her parents until they started to see her in her present state.

While it's OK to hold on to memories of people in our lives, we also need to make space for them to show us who they are today. The codependent in us doesn't want our children to change because it's beyond our control. The perfectionist in us only wants our children to change if it means they're going to do well or be more successful. Transitional parenting requires awareness, presence, and flexibility. When we parent from this place, we allow our children to try different personas, styles, and personalities. We learn to adjust the amount of support and intervention we provide, depending on their changing needs. We take a conscious approach to being with each of our children and determining what they each need in any given moment.

If you practice transitional parenting from when your kids are a young age, then instead of waking up one day and realizing your child is their own person, you witness the slow evolution along the way. This way their eventual adolescence does not shock you. You are more prepared and able to go with the flow of what's happening. In transitional parenting, you slowly allow your child to step up from the early stages of life and into adulthood. I often hear from parents of young adults who ask, *Now what do I do?* But if you've been transitioning with your child, your parenting doesn't need to change, because it's already been constantly shifting. When children hit their late teens, it's a big shift in the parent-child relationship. It's natural to feel grief over what was, but when you take an adaptive approach to parenting, you'll be more prepared when it happens.

THE DIFFERENCE BETWEEN YOU AND ME

Many parents resist the transition into the teenage years and adulthood. But in doing so, they may damage their relationship with their child. Yes, change is very difficult; I say none of this lightly. But change is necessary, and it actually means your child is thriving! Remember, when your child becomes an independent adult, you have done your job well. So, there is a silver lining to some of the loss you may feel as they go their own way. If you let it, this shift can allow for an even more beautiful relationship.

If you resist your child growing into a teen and young adult, the price can be high, including being rejected by your child, or the child not being able to separate from you. Adult children who live with their parents well into adulthood because they can't get jobs to sustain themselves, fear being on their own, or have other inappropriate reasons, usually have parents who have encouraged a dependent relationship. Sadly, this is becoming more common as parents are overly involved and struggle to let go. Dependency in a child-parent relationship is often a matter of comfort for both parties—sometimes more for the parent than the child. But it will quickly become problematic, because the adult child is unable to individuate and gets stuck in an unhealthy dependence. The adult child is still merely a child, rather than a thriving adult.

One of my greatest joys in my therapeutic work was working with a mother who had this type of enmeshed relationship with her adult daughter. Let's take a look.

> At twenty-six years old, Shana was angry with her mother. Not for any one thing she did, but for the long-standing dependency her mother had created with her. Shana's mom had leaned on her as an emotional confidant, especially after her divorce, and Shana resented this. She felt overly responsible for taking care of her mother's emotional (and sometimes other) needs. Shana's mother didn't feel she could depend on her other family and friends for the emotional, physical, and mental support she needed. So, instead she put it primarily on her daughter. But this led to all sorts of problems.

We already understand that in transitional parenting, we naturally decrease the child's dependency on us. But maybe even more importantly, we also need to decrease *our dependency on them*. Remember, our children are not here to take care of us! Children who feel obligated to take care of their parents often live with deep resentment, as Shana did.

It's common for codependent parents to utilize their children to take care of their emotional needs, creating a partner-like relationship with them. But this hurts the child and makes them feel beholden to the parent. Some common examples of unhealthy parental emotional dependency include:

- Speaking to your child about your spouse or ex-spouse excessively or negatively.

- Sharing too much about what's going on for you emotionally.
- Telling your child of your financial woes.
- Telling your child secrets that your actual partner is unaware of.
- Speaking to one child regularly about their sibling.

This puts tremendous stress on children, young and old. I often see adult children struggling with the dependent relationship their parent has created with them, in which they feel they need to always make sure their parent is OK. It can severely impact the mental health of the child, creating anxiety, stress, and even depression. A child should be concerned about their own well-being, and parents should encourage healthy separation and boundaries.

> Going back to Shana, she began resenting her role as mom's caretaker. She started rebelling against her mom in many passive-aggressive ways yet still felt like she couldn't move out because she worried her mom needed *her* too much. This created a negative codependent cycle between them. At one point, Shana even had a panic attack during our work together as she considered what it would feel like not to do as much for her mother. My work with Shana and her mother was not easy, but slowly I helped the mom create a more independent life from her daughter. Once this began to happen, Shana slowly started to heal. Once she felt safer in this new dynamic, she began to lessen her anger and enjoy the time with her mother more. It's amazing what negative emotional bonding can do to sabotage a relationship. These two women now have a much more

> functional, loving, and empathic relationship than they once did, when they felt obligated to one another.

In transitional parenting, we want to *encourage* our children to individuate from us. This is our job! This means that we help them grow less dependent on us, and that we avoid being dependent on them, instead utilizing healthy support from friends and family outside the parent-child relationship. We want to assist them to find themselves and learn who they are. We want them to learn to speak up for themselves (respectfully) and honor how they may be feeling or what they may be thinking. We do not want them to feel responsible for our well-being.

Constantly get to know your children as they grow. We are ever-evolving people; they are, too. Provide space for them to know that they are safe to explore whoever they are. They can discover themselves *with* us if we avoid holding them to some rigid ideal of who we believe they should be. This act of letting go of expectations and assumptions actually allows us to know them better over time, which ultimately leads to a closer, healthier relationship, even when they become independent adults.

REFLECTIVE EXERCISE

Sit in a quiet space with a journal. Consider the following:

My children are constantly evolving. It's my job to discover who they are as they grow in front of me and adjust who I am based on their needs. It's not their job to be responsible for my well-being.

How does this statement differ from how you parent now? Do you need to cut back on what you share? Do you need to be more flexible in how you see your kids? How can you be more in tune with the child in front of you? Spend five minutes writing whatever comes to mind.

CHAPTER 5

HOW TO BE THERE

As you read through this book, be careful not to fall into extremes; as codependents and perfectionists, we tend to either take too much or too little responsibility for things. In the case of taking too much responsibility, some readers may become obsessive about their parenting style and use the information provided here to find all the stuff that they've done *wrong*. As perfectionists, our inner critic is just waiting to judge us for all the things we're not doing well. This could easily lead you to become overwhelmed and give up. That is not my intention!

My goal is to help you see yourself, your child, and your parenting more clearly, and as a result, promote a more authentic, rewarding, and intimate parent-child relationship. Be compassionate—working on yourself as a parent (and a person) is a long road, and there is always time to make changes if you want to. And if you find yourself wishing you had done some things differently, welcome to the club! Just don't be too hard on yourself.

Although in this chapter I discuss the importance of starting this work on your parenting as early as possible, please remember that changes at *any* time are important and can be helpful. Just think of the mom I mentioned with her twenty-six-year-old daughter in the last chapter! So, if you're coming to this a little later in your parenting journey, don't be discouraged. It is all a process. Becoming a better parent is helpful for any child—even an adult child. Regardless of which developmental stage you've reached, making a change to support growth in your relationship with your child is wonderful.

EARLY ATTACHMENT

What many people don't know is that our most impactful parenting happens in the earliest years of our child's life. Although the saying *Bigger kids = bigger problems* is true, what you do during the infant and toddler stages sets the scene for later development.

Think of child development as a house being built. According to John Bowlby (1979), our goals during the infant stage are about attachment. Attachment is an affectionate bond between two individuals that is persistent and emotionally significant (Bowlby, 1979; Ainsworth, Waters, and Wall, 1978). Bowlby's theory states that we come into this world with an instinctual need to connect with our caregivers. He believes that our first year of life is essential in forming this bond between parent and child. He suggests that this relationship forms the way we see the world. Is it safe and secure? Loving? Or rejecting, harsh, and cold? This unconsciously informs how we might interact with the world and within relationships in the future.

Harry Harlow (1958) discovered some remarkable things about attachment in studying rhesus monkeys. In one experiment, Harlow kept baby monkeys from forming any type of attachment by keeping them from an attachment figure for the first few months of life. He found these monkeys had tremendous difficulty relating with others when he introduced them to a larger group of monkeys. They even engaged in odd self-injurious behavior. The damage from the lack of attachment was enduring. In another study, he found that baby rhesus monkeys also strongly preferred a soft cloth surrogate mother opposed to a wire mother who only provided sustenance. This shows it is essential for babies to feel comforted and safe.

Since Bowlby and Harlow, there has been consistent evidence that our primary caregivers and the way they care for us in our early years of life significantly affect how we develop. There's a lot to unpack there, but the most important takeaway is that we want children to develop healthy attachments to their parents or caregivers. The primary way we can create these attachments is by showing consistent love and nurturing. Consistency is probably the most important aspect of care for young children and babies. In its earliest form, that means regularly meeting an infant's basic needs, like eating, diaper changing, and sleeping. Consistency doesn't mean that we have to do something the same way every single time. It means that as parents, we provide babies with a relatively similar experience from day to day so they know that they can rely on us: We will feed them when they are hungry, pick them up in a reasonable amount of time if they show distress, and put them to bed around the same time each day. Now, while consistency is important, I believe that flexibility is also important in order to prevent rigidity on both sides. Some change is healthy.

As I mentioned above, the way we attach early on has been found to inform the way we relate to the world as adults. See model below (taken from Bretherton and Munholland, 1999).

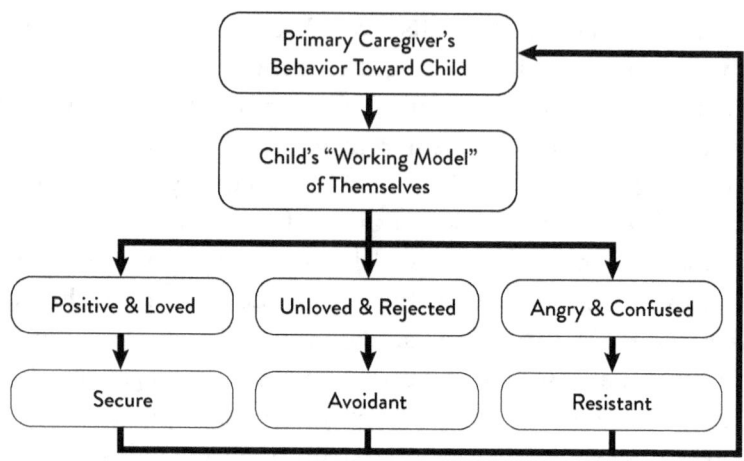

Saul McLeod (2018) (simplypsychology.org) explains that "securely attached children develop a positive working model of themselves and have mental representations of others as being helpful while viewing themselves as worthy of respect (Jacobsen and Hoffman, 1997). Avoidant children think themselves unworthy and unacceptable, caused by a rejecting primary caregiver (Larose and Bernier, 2001). Ambivalent children have a negative self-image and exaggerate their emotional responses as a way to gain attention (Kobak et al., 1993)."

Attachment is like the foundation of a home. As a therapist, I have found that people with effective coping strategies in place are able to navigate traumatic events fairly OK. In the case of people who experienced unstable attachment or early trauma, they tend to have poor coping skills for difficult life experiences. Attachment is the foundation that dictates how we go about weathering life. Sometimes, even a light wind can knock an unstable house off its foundation. When the foundation is strong, the whole house can withstand a major trauma.

As our child moves from infancy into the toddler years, we become important role models. This stage of life is the jewel of child-rearing, when our children begin their first attempts at individuating from us. It is where we set the stage for our child's development. This is the point when we begin to implement boundaries, when we begin to converse with our children as well as hear them (or not), and when we set up our dynamics. This is also often the developmental stage when trauma can be most impactful.

Toddlers are difficult. They are literally and figuratively finding their voice, beginning to speak, and really recognize their separation from us as parents. Toddlers test limits as a means to get to know their caretakers and the world around them. They don't yet have logical thinking but want to do a lot by themselves. They can be stubborn, opinionated, and irrational. As parents, it can be very difficult to know how to handle toddlers. When we're codependent, we're likely to have difficulty allowing our child to find their voice. We may feel too challenged by this voice, leading to us intervening too often, which may begin to silence a child. Or they may act out even further if they feel frustrated with their lack of space to be who they are. We may also have trouble holding space for their emotions at this time. Perfectionists may struggle at this stage, wanting their child to hit all their milestones at the "right" time, trying to find some sense of control. As parents, we want to be mindful of the many anxiety-provoking experiences that can come up during the toddler years and consider if we are there for our child in a balanced way.

Toddlers also need consistency from their parents. They need a fairly predictable schedule, including an age-appropriate bedtime. They need to know their parents will implement boundaries consistently. They need to feel the presence of their parents as they begin to separate. We really need to understand toddlers and their limitations as well as age-appropriate behaviors to make sure we are handling them effectively. Toddlers push our buttons because it's a natural part of their development. It is important to note that if we are too harsh at this time, assuming our child is "acting out," we will likely negatively impact them. Similarly, if we give in too often, we are also likely to give them too much leniency, which can induce anxiety about limits. It's all about finding the balance. Being gentle but firm. Strong but not rigid. Loving but not codependent.

The early years, from zero to five, are a very delicate time in a child's life, and parenting, mixed with our genetics and temperament, sets a person's foundation in life. If you are curious about understanding your own wounds and development during this time, John Bradshaw in his book *Home Coming* presents a series of questions that can give you a deeper understanding of your early trauma.

PREVENTION

I regularly work with parents of teenagers and adults. They often ask me what to do now that their adolescent or adult children have begun to engage in risky behaviors or are presenting serious emotional issues. The truth is that once our children become preteens, most of their primary trauma has happened, and it is more difficult to guide them in becoming their most authentic selves. (More difficult, yes—but still absolutely possible.)

When we're at this point, the work that we need to do is more crisis intervention, rather than prevention. Crisis prevention happens early and over time as we teach, empower, and build up our children to feel safe enough to be who they truly are. Prevention means helping them develop better tools and skills to navigate life's difficulties, but *not* navigating the difficulties for them. When we practice prevention over time, we minimize the necessity for intervention down the line.

According to SAMSA (Substance Abuse and Mental Health Services Administration) (2007), half of all lifetime cases of diagnosable mental illnesses begin by age fourteen. SAMSA also confirms that mental health should be worked on as early as possible in order to prevent mental illness from developing. If you have not yet had children or are the parent of a young child, you'll want to focus on what's called protective factors in prevention by building up your child. Protective factors include teaching your child how to handle conflicts effectively, work through relationship struggles, and solve problems independently.

SAMSA points to parenting as one of the main contributing factors in preventing the development of mental health and substance abuse issues. SAMSA identifies five areas that contribute to building resilience, including family, child, community, school, and peers. It's important to note that some of these factors are directly related to parenting, including many of the following:

Family factors:

- Close relationships with a thoughtful and responsive parent or other caregiver
- Structured and caring parenting
- Socioeconomic advantages
- Connections with supportive family networks
- Small family structure—clear standards of behavior
- Recognition for efforts, improvements, and accomplishments

Child factors:

- Positive temperament
- Good intellectual functioning

- Self-confidence
- Skills that enable a child to participate and succeed in schools
- Faith
- Sense of control over life
- Sense of coherent identity

Sadly, prevention is the most underfunded work in our country. We simply don't invest as people and as a society in preventing issues *before they happen*. When I worked at a substance abuse facility, year after year our funding for prevention would get cut, despite it being proven to be the most impactful of treatments out there. As a society, we instead focus on how we can "fix" issues after the fact. Studies have shown that putting the work in at the beginning (such as prevention work with substance abuse) is more effective than trying to reduce harm after a child has begun to engage in risky behaviors.

Everything in this book comes from my belief that prevention is the most effective strategy for keeping our children healthy, happy, and safe.

THE MASKS WE WEAR

Masks often form when we are not able to be who we really are. A mask can be likened to a false persona that we create to hide our inner worlds and get those around us to see us in a particular way. I believe the creation of a mask begins as early as our first experiences of attachment and continues from there. The creation of a mask happens in reaction to everything from major traumas and how we cope with them to the subtle interactions we have with others. Our parents are our primary role models in life, so they are initially our strongest teachers. They show us how to cope with our emotions, thoughts, and desires. They model this to us most obviously in their behavior, but they also express it to us in our interactions with them. Sometimes what they show us is poise, which teaches us how to handle difficulty with grace. Sometimes what they model is fear, and we unconsciously learn to fear the world.

Close your eyes and think of being a child and crying to your parent, maybe because you scraped your leg or you told your parent something that hurt your feelings. What was the first thing your parents did? What was the first thing your parents said? How did they communicate with you about your pain? Do you remember feeling comforted? One of the most common responses is: *Don't cry.* But think what this might do: Encourage the child to wear a mask to hide their true feelings.

I remember vividly one day when my daughter fell and her mouth was bleeding. In the midst of her crying, a family member turned to me and said, "Well, she'll get used to it; she's a kid." Yes, this is a true statement. However, in the moment, neither of us needed to hear that. Instead we needed to tend to her discomfort. What that family member was really saying was, she'll stop having feelings over it eventually and it'll be OK. It was simply too quick to go to this place. What I believe my daughter needed in that moment was just the comfort of a loving embrace until she felt OK enough to move on.

When we move too quickly to stop our children's feelings, we inadvertently give them the message that they should change their emotions or stop feeling. Most often children create a mask to show that they don't actually feel the way they are feeling on the inside because they need to "be a big boy" and "grow up." I'm not sure when "grow up" became synonymous with "stop feeling," but it's very indicative of the society we live in.

If you already have children, you may be thinking, *I'm not a monster and haven't done anything traumatic to my children by telling them not to cry. I was just trying to be helpful!* I'm sure you were! There's no dispute that we may have the best intentions when we are parenting; however, that doesn't mean our approach is the most beneficial for the child. If you're already a parent of a child who is a toddler or older, try sitting with your child the next time they get upset and try not doing anything to alleviate it. Don't tell them it will be OK. Just offer a hug and be with them through it. Boy, is that tough!

It's very important to examine how your codependency and perfectionism may affect your children when you want them to be a certain type of person or act in a particular way. Again, one of the best ways to help your child be who they really are is to show it to them by example rather than attempt to control them. Start this as early as you can. The earlier you begin to see parenting through a preventative lens, the more likely your child will not develop the need to wear a mask in the home. This means they have more space to be free, explore who they are, feel their feelings, and learn how to cope with feelings effectively.

REFLECTIVE EXERCISE

Let's take a look at your mask!

- How do you think others perceive you?
- What are you holding back from showing or sharing with them?
- What's your first memory of "putting on" this mask?
- How has it served you not to show others these parts of yourself?

OR

List three ways you can utilize prevention with your children right now to build them up. Be specific and implement these ways!

CHAPTER 6

TAKE A STEP BACK

Children are resilient by nature. (Thank God!) Still, we want to guide them to become as resilient as possible over time. In my practice, I often work with adults who have limited abilities to work through challenges. They generally don't have a strong sense of self and struggle with decisions like which career to pursue or person to date. These adults often end up becoming highly apathetic. They tend to have unrealistic expectations about what life should be, and they aren't excited about many aspects of their present situation. Eventually many of them give up entirely. In my work with these people, I observe a lack of the resilience needed to navigate the natural ups and downs of life. In many cases, "helicopter parenting" has played a big role in their issues.

Helicopter parenting is when a parent continually swoops in to take care of—or rescue—their children. These parents consistently "drop in" to save their children from challenges.

The *New York Times* article "How Parents Are Robbing Their Children of Adulthood" (2019), which came out shortly after the college admissions scandal, argued that parents today are moving from helicopter parenting to *snowplow parenting*, meaning they don't just rescue but try to remove any difficulties from their children's way altogether. This demonstrates that this issue is only getting worse, not better!

Both helicopter and snowplow parenting are linked to codependency and perfectionism. The key link to codependency is the parent's discomfort with allowing their child to face difficult experiences (such as not getting into college), while the perfectionism has to do with making sure their child can succeed and appear to meet society's expectations. The college admissions scandal is a great example of codependency and perfectionism in action, with parents going to great lengths, even committing crimes, to make sure their child is accepted into the "right" college. These parents are literally willing to put their own freedom at risk for their child's perceived success. The codependent way of parenting is detrimental for many reasons, but most of all because it cheats our children of learning how to cope with life and build self-esteem. Sadly, this can set them up for failure as adults.

Both helicopter parents and snowplow parents are in codependent habits and living in fear. They fear their children experiencing any discomfort. They fear their children looking *less than*. These parents believe that in their efforts to shield their children, they are "saving" them from pain. This sets up an unrealistic experience of life, one where problems magically disappear, which leads to an inability to cope with life on life's terms as adults in the real world. Instead of supporting them, these codependent parents unintentionally send their children the message, *You can't handle things on your own.*

SUPPORT OR SHIELDING?

The reality is that life is filled with many challenging and painful experiences. None of us can avoid this. If your child doesn't learn how to deal with them from an early age, how will they ever learn? Support and shielding are two very different things. When we actually support our children in their development, we help steer them through adversity (and try not to be the ones bringing adversity into their lives). But trying to eliminate *any* difficulty or trauma for your child can create longstanding issues. It's important for children to learn how to cope with difficulties. As parents, we can help them through by modeling how to do this when challenges arise in our own lives.

One of my favorite parenting writers, M. Scott Peck, states in his book *The Road Less Traveled*:

> Therefore let us inculcate in ourselves and in our children the means of achieving mental and spiritual health. By this I mean let us teach ourselves and our children the necessity for suffering and the value thereof, the need to face problems directly and to experience the pain involved.

He goes on to discuss how coping with life stressors allows us to build discipline, an especially important skill for adults.

Many of my codependent parent clients say, *But isn't it my job to help them and make them feel better? Why wouldn't I stop them from experiencing pain if I could?* Then these parents go on to make it their job to tell their children what to do in almost every situation in order to avoid any difficult consequences.

Sure, I would love for every kid to make the best decisions for their future at all times. However, that's not only completely unrealistic, but it also deprives them of the natural growth process—something codependency loves to rob people of. We like to take away problems instead of helping our children learn how to navigate those problems themselves. Making suggestions and providing guidance is absolutely fine and appropriate, but check in with yourself. It's one thing to provide someone a suggestion once, maybe twice. Then it's time to back off. You do not need to tell your child a hundred times why college is important or smoking pot is bad for them or why they need to do their homework. In fact, the more you tell your children the same thing, the less they listen! So, choose your interventions wisely and let them face their own consequences and subsequently learn from them.

We want our home to be a safe place for our children to explore themselves and get support. Talk to your children about what they're going through. Make the home a place to explore feelings, discuss emotions, and learn how to cope with the inevitable pain that will come their way. Teach them that it is understandable to be disappointed, hurt, or sad when we are let down, don't win the game, or have a fight with a friend, but don't stop them from feeling or try to change their feelings. This is how they learn to cope. Give them the words to speak with friends, teachers, or coaches about their feelings. It is OK to help them find even more encouragement than you can provide alone. Your job is only to make sure they get the support they need.

REFLECTIVE EXERCISE

Stop helicoptering!

Make a commitment to take a step back three times in the coming week. Every time you feel yourself wanting to intervene, take a pause and ask yourself, "Would it be better if I let my child handle this? Could it somehow be helpful for their self-esteem to work through this issue without me?" It can be something as small as letting them keep trying to grab something they can't reach or as big as facing a difficulty in a relationship. Journal about each experience and how it felt for you as a parent. Reflect on how your child reacted and navigated the challenge.

CHAPTER 7

CONSEQUENCES & BOUNDARIES

Before we dive into this topic, let me be clear: I'm not saying that children shouldn't face consequences for their behavior; they absolutely should. The problem is that many codependents do not let their kids experience appropriate consequences. As codependents, we are likely to feel our children's feelings as our own, so it's tough to let our child feel pain or disappointment, and we might not let them experience consequences when appropriate. Because of this, we enable negative behavior. Let me share a quick anecdote to illustrate this dynamic.

> Joshua, a twenty-five-year-old man, had been in and out of about six treatment programs by the time I first met with him and his mother, Jean. He had been a few

months clean from substance use then, and I was working on some relationship issues between him and Jean. While I was trying to point out to Jean that Joshua didn't agree with her codependent behavior, he brought up a time when he got in trouble at school and his privileges to leave the school for study hall were suspended. His mother fought to have these privileges restored, but she didn't win. Joshua was required to stay in study hall alone at school while his friends left. Instead of allowing her son to experience this consequence, Jean decided that she would meet her son during this period every day so he didn't have to be alone. She felt this "solution" was helping her son because he had been very hurt by not being allowed to go out for his free period.

Jean explained to Joshua why she did it. She reminded him that at the time, he was very upset about the punishment. She felt the school was treating him unfairly, so she decided that this was the best thing to do. Joshua remarked, "Of course I was upset about it. I was thirteen! But I was acting out, and if the school said I shouldn't be allowed to go out, maybe they were right!" In the child's view, the mother was unknowingly undermining the school system's use of consequences. He also resented his mother for not enforcing the boundaries he felt he needed!

This is a great example of a parent who felt they were doing right by their child, only to have their child actually resent the parent's decision to step in and not allow them to experience consequences. Of course, there are times when we'll need to stand up for our children when something is not OK. For example, if they are being discriminated against, violated, or in some way harmed, especially by an authority figure. Jean felt that this was what was going on here, but interestingly, Joshua didn't. As parents, we need to understand the difference between not wanting our children to experience appropriate consequences and noticing if something happens to them that is not acceptable.

BOUNDARIES

Children want and need boundaries, which include consequences for particular behaviors. We really set the stage for this in the earliest years of a child's life. By the end of toddlerhood, a child has a good idea of the limits they're working with. If you don't enforce limits in these early years, it will get really tough to do so down the road. So, do your best to enforce, enforce, enforce, while also leaving lots of room for your children to explore within these boundaries. Children love to plead and try to get their way. This is natural. But you are the parent, and it's your job to set boundaries and uphold them. It's not enough to *say* you're setting a limit. You always need to follow through so your kids know the boundaries are secure.

I also want to clarify that there's a big difference here between changing your mind about a boundary and giving up on implementing one. A boundary can change, but if you simply don't follow through on a limit you've set, that teaches your child to push harder, knowing you're likely going to give up eventually. This scenario is common with codependent parents, who have difficulty withstanding the pushback they get from their kids for saying no, which then leads to them saying yes. Children know when we can't stand their emotional outbursts, and they're likely to have more of them when they know it causes us to give in eventually. Supportive parents understand why their child might be upset about a boundary but don't feel the need to change it because of this. Codependents are more likely to get frustrated, annoyed, or upset with their child for having feelings about boundaries and limits, leading them to just give up or lash out.

When a boundary changes, you need to explain why. For example: "I know I told you that you can't go to parties in the evenings if you haven't gone to school that day. You've really respected that rule, and I appreciate that. I can see that you really weren't feeling well earlier, but now you feel much better, so I've decided to change this rule just this once." This is very different from a kid asking you twenty-five times to go to the party knowing the rule but relentlessly trying to get you to give in to what they want. Eventually you feel so depleted that you just say, "Fine, go to the party!" That only teaches them that your boundaries are weak.

NATURAL CONSEQUENCES

Pete Walker, in his book *Complex PTSD: From Surviving to Thriving*, states, "Enlightened parents introduce limits slowly but surely." The toddler stage is when we really begin to teach. Before that, we are ensuring survival, providing love, and working on healthy attachment with our child. Once it's time to start introducing boundaries and consequences, parents might get overwhelmed or confused. There is no manual describing exactly how to go about this with a toddler, but doing so is extremely important and impactful. The key is setting appropriate boundaries and consequences for children while not shaming or punishing them.

All consequences should be age-appropriate and based on the issue at hand. For example, with a toddler, a consequence for not sharing may be that you take the toy away and give it to the other child until it's their turn again. Consequences are so important because they teach children that certain behaviors will result in an outcome that they don't like. This corresponds well to real life. For example, if they show up late to work as adults, they may get fired. You want your child to understand that this is how things work and teach them to consider consequences before they act. "Protecting" them from the pain of a consequence ultimately doesn't do them any favors.

I am not in favor of consequences that are not directly correlated to the behavior at hand. For example, grounding your child for not doing their homework. This type of result tends to be more about trying to have power over your child than allowing them to experience a consequence of their behavior (which might be getting a bad grade or an "incomplete" on the assignment). Perfectionists might be sweating while reading that, and codependents might struggle to watch their child have feelings that come along with not doing well in school, but the reality is that we have to allow our child to experience what happens based on their actions.

Let's take a look at a father and daughter duo I worked with extensively on boundaries and consequences.

> Sam came to see me after his daughter, Lily (seventeen), had gone through a series of treatment programs for substance abuse and mental health. He was at his wit's end with his daughter. She had stopped being respectful to Sam and had decided that she was going to leave the house and move in with her boyfriend because she didn't like Sam's rules, which included her having to be clean. Sam didn't know what to do. He didn't want his daughter to move out, but he also couldn't have her living in his home and not respecting his rules. Sam decided to let his daughter go. I encouraged Sam to establish strict boundaries with Lily if he was going to let her leave. Sam agreed.

> He told her, "I will let you go, but if you leave my home, I will not pay for your expenses. I will still support your medical costs, but that's it. You can come home at any time if you change your mind." Then came the hard work of Sam actually having to implement his boundaries. There were many days when Sam came to me in tears, saying things like, "I can't let her struggle like this. She's calling me saying she's hungry. I feel like I need to give her something!" But he kept at it, enforcing his boundaries and allowing her to experience the consequences of her decision. It was a long road with a lot of trials and tribulations, but Sam stuck to his boundaries. Several years later, Lily is the better for it. They now have a pleasant relationship where they respect each other, and Lily is able to appreciate the boundaries Sam put into place many years ago. She no longer actively struggles with substance abuse and continues living with her boyfriend.

This example illustrates that natural consequences are really the best of all consequences. A natural consequence of moving out of your parents' home is that you need to get a job to support yourself. A small, everyday example is telling your child to wear warmer clothes because it is cold out, and if they refuse to do so, they will have to experience what it feels like to be cold all day. Remember, none of us want our children to have negative experiences, but it is important for children to understand what happens when they make particular decisions without their parents protecting them or enforcing unrelated consequences. The earlier you can get in the habit of this, the better.

TEACHING VERSUS PUNISHMENT

Guides do not punish, they teach. When we see teaching as our role as parents, we get to enjoy our positions of authority more. When we punish, there's an unspoken message of shame: *You're bad*. But when a child "does something wrong," we need to look at our goal: Do we want them to feel bad about themselves, or do we want them to learn from their behavior? If your goal is for your child to simply not do it again, then you are in a punishment mindset and may be unknowingly more focused on making them feel bad in the moment. If your goal is to help your child understand their behavior and how it impacts themselves and others, then you are in a teaching mindset that sets them up to do better next time. Teaching is about guiding and mentoring.

Shame is too often used as a tool to try to make children achieve more or be different. Statements such as *If you weren't so lazy you'd get good grades* are meant to be motivators, but they are actually shame-inducing statements that suggest there is something wrong with the *person*. Punishments for bad grades, such as grounding your child or taking away things they enjoy, can also send the message that your child is bad. As Brené Brown explains in *Daring Greatly*, "Shame is positively correlated with addiction, depression, aggression, violence, eating disorders, and suicide, and . . . guilt is inversely correlated with these outcomes." Shame is never effective. We never want someone to believe in any way that they are less than. The distinction for parents is in identifying negative behaviors—as opposed to identifying the person—as negative. For example, trying to understand why your child may not be putting their full effort into school rather than lashing out and calling them lazy. We address this type of language in more depth in Chapter 13.

When we are teaching instead of punishing, we assume that children aren't purposely acting out to torture us. (Although it may feel that way sometimes!) We remember that they are generally good and loving, and we try to guide them in this direction as we address a negative behavior. If we do this, we are less likely to punish out of our own frustration and more likely to introduce limits and boundaries that help our children get back to their good and loving nature.

Physical punishment is something that I could never understand until becoming a parent myself. I knew the intellectual aspect of it but never felt empathy for people who punish their children in this way. I now know what it feels like to have every bone in my body want to lash out at my child because it feels like they are torturing me. Although I've never hit my child, because I strongly disagree with it, I can understand how people get to this point. It takes all the strength in me not to lash out sometimes. However, physical punishment has been studied at length, and time and again the results suggest that it is not helpful. I firmly believe that corporal punishment is not an appropriate consequence for negative behavior and ultimately instills fear in your child.

There may be times when force is needed to calm or stop your child (such as yanking them out of the way of a moving car), but physically lashing out is different and is about us, not our children. Physical punishment is always a power move. A move to intimidate and garner fear. The problem is, it doesn't work. If you want your child to fear you when they're young, it may work for behavioral changes in the moment, but you will likely lose the respect and trust of your child over time. Physical punishment also teaches children to be physical and more prone to violence. Be mindful of relying too heavily on short-term solutions instead of doing the work that provides long-term benefit.

As M. Scott Peck stated, "Good discipline requires time. When we have no time to give our children, or no time that we are willing to give, we don't even observe them closely enough to become aware of when their need for our disciplinary assistance is expressed subtly"(*The Road Less Traveled*, p. 22). We live busy lives, and Peck goes on to say that we often don't even have the energy to deal with disciplining our children, which requires both time and skill. I get this. Some of my earliest experiences disciplining my children took a lot of time! I remember both of my kids throwing tantrums, which led to me spending almost an hour redirecting them to pick up food that they had thrown on the floor.

Throwing food on the floor is something most infants and young toddlers will do; they aren't acting maliciously. But as toddlers grow up, it can be helpful for them to understand that when they throw something, they need to pick it up themselves. There's no reason to punish a child for doing this or yell at them (both of which will induce shame). However, the reason I spent an hour redirecting my children back to pick up the food is because I knew that if I didn't enforce the boundary from the beginning, they wouldn't respect the boundary over time. The limit I set was: *You throw the food, you pick it up.* But if you don't have the time or energy to enforce this type of consequence, you're better off not even trying. I firmly believe that a consequence not enforced is worse than no consequence.

When we spend the time with our children while they are young, teaching them, guiding them, helping them understand, we can prevent the need for more serious interventions in the teenage years. By then our hard work in many ways will be done. Most parents of teenagers would say, *No way! This is where the hard work begins!* Nope, not if we've really taken the time when they're young to guide and teach them. If that doesn't make the effort worth it, I don't know what does!

Recently, I was watching Whoopi Goldberg interview a celebrity on *The View*. She asked him how it was having a teenage daughter and if he felt that difficulty that most parents feel about having teenagers. To the audience's surprise (and mine), he said, "No, I love it! She's great, and I'm really enjoying this phase with her." Wow, you don't hear that often. It's great when a parent can truly enjoy any phase of life with their children. This is my wish for you, to enjoy your experience with your children at every step of the way.

HOW TO TEACH

First of all, talk *with* your child—not *at* them—often. Try to understand why they may have acted a particular way. Ask them lots of questions! Explain yourself and the reasons you make the decisions you do. Talk about why certain behaviors aren't OK (because they may hurt someone else's feelings, they could cause physical harm, etc.). Good teachers connect with their students first. This means they put the relationship with their students above the material. They know that without a solid connection, children will act out and be less likely to take in the information. Most of all, children want to feel loved, seen, and cared for. Talking with them in the ways described above will help build and foster your relationship, even while enforcing consequences.

For young children:

- Use plain, easy-to-understand language.
- Make sure they understand what you've said by checking in with them afterward and asking what they heard.

- Use examples relevant to their life experience and people or characters they know. (For example, Cookie Monster also needs to be patient, which means he knows he has to wait for the cookies to be ready before he eats them.)
- Don't assume they understand how things work—they usually don't.
- Help them identify language that they can use to express themselves. Teach them words by repeating yourself regularly and asking questions. Also, research suggests that sign language can be helpful for preverbal children.
- Assume they have good intentions but limited ability to cope with their feelings and to express themselves.
- Acknowledge them often for their efforts and show appreciation when they do something helpful, kind, or positive. Be mindful not to only react to the negative!

For preteens or older:

- Don't be condescending. Try to speak with them in an adult manner while being age-appropriate with the content.
- Plant seeds. Don't assume that what you teach will manifest at lighting speed. Picture it more like a garden that needs to be sowed, watered, and nurtured until you eventually reap the harvest.
- Share your own experiences and how you've struggled to help them relate to you on a human level.
- Try to understand their perspective before deciding something is "bad" or "wrong."

- Don't assume that because they argue or fight back that they aren't getting it—some of my most combative clients are the best learners.
- Acknowledge them often for their efforts and show appreciation.

Let's look at some examples of what teaching looks like in real life.

Billy is a three-year-old boy who consistently throws tantrums when he gets frustrated. We want to teach Billy two things: how to express himself more effectively and how to calm himself down. This could involve talking to Billy when he is not upset, asking something like, "Billy, what's your favorite toy or stuffed animal that helps you feel safe?" Once he shows you, you could practice what it looks like to use that as a calming method. Help him learn how to breathe as he holds his special security object. Tell him you're there to give him a hug whenever he needs it. Then, give him some new words or ways he can show you what's wrong using motions, hand signs, and pictures to help him express himself before he gets to the tantrum level.

Thomas is a fourteen-year-old boy who is failing history. The urge as a parent, especially a codependent perfectionist, is to either fix this somehow for him or to punish him for failing. But the best thing to do is to find out the *why*: Why is he failing? Once we find this out, we can actually support Thomas. Could we find a way to help him navigate the material differently? Does he need more visuals because that's how he learns? We want to coach Thomas in how he can speak with his teacher about what's going on and find out what he can do about it without rescuing or punishing him. We also want to accept that our child may not be good at everything, and that's OK too!

TEACHING EMPATHY

Young children don't have a natural ability to empathize with others. Meaning, they can't simply put themselves in someone else's shoes to understand another's emotional experience. One of the ways teaching can be helpful is to guide your child to try to understand how their actions could hurt someone else. You want to be mindful not to shame your child in this moment by asking questions like, *How could you do that to Simon?* Instead, ask, *What do you think Simon might feel if you take that toy from him? How would you feel if Simon did that to you?* This guides your child into beginning to think about others.

At the same time, you want to teach your child that they're not responsible for the other person's feelings and emotional experience (to discourage codependency). The balance is in helping them understand how their behavior can contribute to another person's feelings. We don't want them to feel like they also need to fix or eliminate the other person's feelings, but taking responsibility for their own behavior and truly understanding its impact is key.

MORE THAN "FINE"

The response I most commonly get when I share my views about teaching is something like, *Well, my parents did ____ and I turned out fine.* Sound familiar? Usually the blank is something clearly not great like spanking or being overly strict. While, sure, many of these people *did* turn out fine, think about it: Don't you want more for your kids than just turning out fine? This approach is about helping our children thrive and grow into their best selves. It's about moving away from the societal pressure of codependent and perfectionist parenting so we can keep them closer to who they really are. It's also about creating loving relationships that will always flourish. And about helping us enjoy our time with them. There's so much more to life than "fine"!

> **REFLECTIVE EXERCISE**
>
> Sitting with your journal, identify at least three times you have gotten in the way of your child experiencing a natural consequence. It may be an experience such as them falling or a time when you did their homework for them so that they didn't get a zero on the assignment. Write about the experience and what came up for you during that time. Fear? Frustration? Sadness? Write about what might have happened if you hadn't stepped in and why this may have been helpful for your child.

CHAPTER 8

NAVIGATING YOUR POWER

Power dynamics pop up in any relationship where one person is the authority and the other person is subordinate (for lack of a better word). Children are inherently subordinate to their parents from the day they are born. This sets up what I'll call parent privilege. But if children feel powerless in their position, they are more likely to rebel against the repression they feel or continue a cycle of repression in their lives. Therefore, we want our children to feel empowered while still respecting authority and understanding that they won't always get their way.

As I mentioned earlier, punishment is a move of power in which a parent clearly asserts their authority over their child. The more effective path forward is to empower our children to speak up for themselves as appropriate. We can help our children do this by inviting open dialogue with them in our own homes and taking the time to hear them out. Try to understand their point even if you don't agree. Sometimes we may even change our opinion as a result of hearing our kid out!

It's also natural for a child to try to gain power in their relationship with their parents. It's developmentally appropriate for children to assert themselves, trying to find their voice and rule the roost. However, it's important for a parent to maintain a position of authority within their family. Remember, children need and want boundaries, and it's your responsibility as the parent to create these—even if your kids put up a good fight or two. They test you, but they need you to remain a consistent authority figure in order to feel safe. It seems contradictory both to remain in power and to empower our children, but there are ways to go about doing this!

THE RULER OF YOUR KINGDOM

Let's consider that you are the queen or king of your land. To promote optimal growth for your people, what type of ruler would you want to be? If we become a dictatorship in which our people have no say and are simply seen as underlings, it's likely that the community will not thrive. This causes unnecessary dependency. A queen or king of this type would say something like, *We do it this way because I said so!* without further explanation. There's no teaching in this type of dictatorship. Instead, the ruler wants to keep their people dependent on their absolute authority.

As parents, we don't often realize that many of our rules are arbitrary. I challenge you to think about why you may want things to be one way. If the answer is *Because I say so*, then I would consider getting rid of that rule. But if you have a real reason, such as *If you ate only potato chips every day, you would not get the nutrition you need*, you have a strong reason to keep the rule and explain it to your child.

Now, what if as a ruler you agree to take into consideration your people's needs when making an important decision? This leads to a more fair society, where the people feel included, heard, and connected. Similarly, we can include our children in decisions. This is a wonderful way to make them feel heard and seen. A small example of how to do this is giving your child some options about what to have for dinner (if you have the time, space, and energy for this). Get them involved in what you're making and let them help. Another example would be allowing your teenager to determine their own curfew. Let them give you a good argument for why they believe it should be a certain time. If they have a good reason and you trust them, go for it.

Remember, in a thriving society, the people wouldn't rule *over* the queen or king, but they would feel represented and involved. In a happy kingdom, the people trust their leader. They don't just see them as some distant person in power who rules their life. They aren't always happy with the decisions they make, but they ultimately trust and respect them. This is the dynamic we're after as parents.

PARENTS' FEELINGS

Children want their parents to be happy. When parents are struggling with their own feelings, children tend to believe those feelings are about them. Now, I'm not saying parents can never feel or express anything negative. We're humans; we're going to have a range of feelings, both positive and negative. But think carefully about how you deal with your feelings. How do you speak to your children about your negative feelings? Do you say things like, *Mommy had a bad day at work and she's tired*? Or do you come home in a bad mood and sit quietly or angrily at the dinner table? When we do things like this with no explanation, our children feel confused and assume it is their fault. Then they might try to change the way we feel, like by being extraquiet so as not to disturb us, or making jokes to lighten the mood. When children do this, they are learning to have codependent habits with us. We need our children to know that they are not responsible for our well-being.

An example of this is one of my clients, who stated, "I learned how to be manipulatively cute." At an early age, she learned she could make her family happy with her cuteness. If you met this particular client, you would most likely think she is lovely, because she is! Unfortunately, some of this loveliness isn't coming from authentic expression but from a manipulative survival tactic. She learned to act this way for the benefit of others, but what she *really* wants is the freedom to be herself without feeling responsible for the feelings of others.

The lesson here is that if we want to teach our children to do what's right, to be who and what they want to be, and to learn from their behavior, we don't want them doing certain things just to please us. When a child feels responsible for their parents' feelings, they can have various difficulties later in life, one of which is reenacting this in their other relationships.

CULTURAL, SOCIETAL, RELIGIOUS, & FAMILY NORMS

It is our job as leaders to look at why we believe what we believe. Most of our beliefs are rooted in the cultural, societal, religious, and family norms that have surrounded us throughout our life. Sometimes these traditions and norms are wonderful and provide a beautiful foundation, but sometimes they are confining and even destructive. It's up to us to examine these influences and decide what works for us. This can be scary at first, but it's a crucial step in becoming an aware and authentic leader.

Many of the norms we grow up with are meant to be helpful. And many are! For instance, I grew up with a tradition of Sunday family dinners. I loved how everyone got together on Sundays to eat, talk, and enjoy each other's company. It taught me about meaningful family bonding as a child and is a tradition I think is important to carry on in some way with my own children. But where we can get into trouble is if we don't leave room for these norms to evolve. For example, growing up with physical punishment in your home. I've had many people say to me that it's normal for them to hit their children, based on their own upbringing. While this is somewhat logical, it's still our job to reexamine these norms and determine what's helpful and what may be hurtful. Similarly, some cultures believe that children shouldn't have a voice, that they should *be seen and not heard.* If we don't question these norms, we can maintain the status quo of mistreatment and abuse.

If you're setting a limit and have no idea why you're doing it, take a moment and examine where it came from. Ask yourself, *Is this something my mother or father used to do? Has this just been passed down? Is it a cultural or religious norm?* If so, was it effective? If not, it may be time to let it go. Question yourself, and let your children question you as well. We should not expect our children to automatically believe what we believe. We must be comfortable letting them think for themselves. Otherwise, we may stifle them.

Let's look at a client of mine who grew up with a strong desire to please his father and grandfather by following their religious desires.

> Ernie was brought up in an Orthodox Jewish household, but his mother was not Jewish and had not converted.

From the beginning, he received some confusing messages about adhering to the faith. The family practiced some aspects of the religion very seriously and others not as much. Ernie came to see me because he struggled with low self-esteem. He also had a problem with marijuana, which he used excessively. One day he came in and stated, "Alana, I just don't know how I feel about being an Orthodox Jew. I've spent my whole life trying to please my father and grandfather by being a 'good Jew,' but the truth is that I don't even know how I actually feel about it." Ernie not only didn't have a strong sense of his religion, but he had almost no sense of self because he spent most of his life trying to please his family by practicing the religion appropriately, which "made them happy." This is codependency; this is an example of a child doing something to please his parents at the expense of himself.

The point of this story isn't that we shouldn't pass down our cultural, religious, or moral beliefs to our children. We absolutely can and should! It's about how the way we do it matters. Are we doing it in a way that makes our children feel they have no choice except to do what we want? Or in a way that provides them the necessary space to explore and make their own choices?

Codependency is such a pervasive issue in our society. I cannot tell you the number of clients who come to me struggling to choose between their parents' desires and wishes and their own. The saddest thing is that these people usually think choosing their own way will jeopardize their relationships with their parents. They feel so responsible for their parents' feelings, they are scared to do what feels right for them, which holds them back from being their best, most authentic selves.

REFLECTIVE EXERCISE

What was considered "normal" in your household? List ten norms you grew up with. They could be things like *Don't speak about anger* or *If you speak up, you get punished.* Let yourself identify the norms you would like to keep and those you would like to change or eliminate. Reflect on the ways this would be good for you and your family.

CHAPTER 9

AGE-APPROPRIATE BEHAVIOR

I recently read an article in which a parent described how much easier it was having their second child because they knew that what their child was doing was normal since they had already been through it. Imagine if we didn't need to use our older children as guinea pigs to learn what's normal? Of course, all children are different, but still, if we don't understand age-appropriate behavior, we might mistake normal development for bad behavior. This could cause us to punish our child when they only need to be guided.

To learn about age-appropriate behavior, check in with your pediatrician regularly, ask lots of questions, and find out if what your child is doing is consistent with a range of behaviors at their age. Read books about child development. Also, ask friends. Join support groups or new parent groups. You'll find out so much this way, and it can really help put your mind at ease.

If we don't understand a behavior as age-appropriate, we may shame a child for something they actually have little or no control over. For example, expecting a two-year-old to carry a full cup of water with no top on it without spilling it. Or assuming if we lend our car to a teen that they will take care of it just as we would. I've also heard of parents giving responsibilities to children who were simply too young to carry them out well (or at all), such as having a five-year-old do her own laundry. We need to understand that our children are simply not capable of the same behavior adults are. It's recently been found that the brain continues to develop until around age twenty-five! This means that even at the age of twenty-one, when we're considered a full adult, we don't necessarily have the same thinking capacities as an older adult.

> Emily, a thirty-five-year-old client of mine, has trauma from her childhood experiences of growing up in a home with an overly harsh and critical mother. She recounts one time when she was around five years old and accidentally spilled milk all over the table. Her mother jumped up and began screaming at her. Emily was terrified and internalized this experience to mean there was something wrong with her that she could be so clumsy, even though she wasn't clumsy—she was just five!

We really want to be mindful of the way we react to our children when they are just being children. At the same time, just because something is age-appropriate doesn't mean you say, OK, *it's fine,* and then leave it alone. In fact, these can be crucial moments when you need to pay attention to the right way to deal with a particular behavior. For example, it is appropriate for toddlers to assert themselves and try to figure out how far they can push the envelope. This is not fun for parents whose kids are this age; but in general, a child of this age shouldn't be punished for being assertive.

Another more controversial example is that it is normal for toddlers to begin masturbating. If you don't think this is normal, then you'll probably have a strong reaction to it. As explained in the book *Counseling Individuals Through the Lifespan* by Wong, Hall, Justice, and Hernandez, it "is normal and should not be punished, but a parent may wish to redirect the child to masturbate in a private setting. A parent's reaction (including voice, word choice, and facial expressions) is the child's greatest lesson regarding sexuality." One's reaction can unknowingly have a big impact on the child's exploration of his or her sexuality down the line.

Another important example of age-appropriate behavior is teenagers who say things that can feel really hurtful to their parents. We need to be careful about reacting to these behaviors from our bruised ego and instead try to understand why our teens may have spoken to us in this way. It's not that we have to accept it and let it go, but it's important not to get too caught up in any one particular statement from a teen who is just naturally finding their independence.

DEVELOPMENT THROUGH THE YEARS

To better understand age-appropriate behaviors, let's take a look at psychologist Erik Erikson's stages of psychosocial development. This provides the big picture of how we develop over the years. Although Erikson's stages span one's entire life, for the sake of this book, we'll just look at child development through young adulthood.

According to Erikson, each stage of life presents a crisis that we either overcome or continue to struggle with. Children grow rapidly between zero and twelve years old and experience many stages during this time. Adults need to understand what is important for their child to learn during these times in order to encourage—not impede—the growth process.

The following chart explains the main stages of human development according to Erikson. As you can see, Erikson presents the information in a simplified nature that doesn't account for cultural differences. It is a very generalized approach but provides a loose idea of what goes on in each particular stage of child development, which is helpful for all parents.

ERIKSON'S STAGES OF PSYCHOSOCIAL DEVELOPMENT

Approximate Age	Psychosocial Crisis
Infant–18 months	Trust vs. Mistrust
18 months–3 years	Autonomy vs. Shame and Doubt
3–5 years	Initiative vs. Guilt
5–13 years	Industry vs. Inferiority
13–21 years	Identity vs. Role Confusion
21–39 years	Intimacy vs. Isolation
40–65 years	Generativity vs. Stagnation
65 and older	Integrity vs. Despair

© The Psychology Notes Headquarter – http://www.PsychologyNotesHQ.com

Erikson's theory is that during each stage, we have the opportunity to either successfully navigate the changes or not. Our ability to progress through the challenges inherent in each stage of development is connected to our later success in life. (And by success, I don't mean having money, but becoming a functioning adult.) He calls the challenge of each stage a "psychosocial crisis." Although we do not need to accomplish one stage to go to the next one, if we are unable to successfully overcome the challenge within a stage, we are likely to bring issues with us and have more difficulty as we continue to develop. We will likely get stuck in some way.

As we've explored in earlier chapters, in the first stage of life, we are working on attaching to a caregiver. As Erikson says, we need to know we have adults we can trust. So, from birth to eighteen months, the main developmental crisis is Trust vs. Mistrust. Caregivers who are not responsive enough to their infant's needs can begin to create within them feelings of anxiety, fear, and distrust. This distrust can then evolve into mistrust for all people later in life. You'll see adults like this with thick walls up that keep them from truly connecting with those around them. I've seen many clients with attachment issues, who have a very difficult time in relationships. Often, we don't have a lot of information about this early stage of life, but the impact of poor attachment can be pretty evident in how a client connects (or more appropriately, doesn't connect) with those around them. The importance of this first stage cannot be stressed enough.

In Autonomy vs. Shame & Doubt, the crisis occurring in Erikson's second stage of development, a toddler is beginning to develop a sense of who they are. They start to see themselves as independent from those around them and begin to have their own preferences. They want to do things *by myself!* (as my toddler demands). In this stage, children are explorers in a vast world. They are working to develop a sense of autonomy.

The input of a parent is crucial here. I see a lot of parents who don't understand how impactful this phase is in a child's development. They think of the child as being obstinate. And they are, but only in an effort to discover themselves. The crucial challenge in this phase is whether the child can learn to trust their own autonomy or they feel they need to consistently bend to the wishes and desires of their parent.

This is when a child really begins to recognize they are distinct from their parents. They want to do things by themselves and feel like a grown-up. They want to be as autonomous as possible, which can be really challenging for us parents. But we want to make sure to help them feel independent, give them the ability to make decisions, and encourage them to feel good about their new capabilities. If we deny these opportunities, we may teach our child that they are not capable, which can lead to the experience of shame and doubt over a lifetime.

According to Erikson, a child who successfully navigates this stage will have a sense of confidence in exploring the world. They will begin to form an identity or sense of self that is closest to who they are. A child who doesn't navigate this phase successfully may struggle to understand who they are and what they like. They may not try different ways of dressing, for example, but instead stick with whatever their parents told them to wear. They may become fearful to test out new things like foods, opinions, or activities. They'll tend to play it safe. I often hear people overdoing *Be careful!* in this phase, which makes their child fearful of the world. Saying *Be careful* is obviously necessary at times, but try to do it sparingly!

The next crisis, occurring between three and five, is Initiative vs. Guilt. In this stage, children are hopefully beginning to really feel a sense of self. They have a desire to learn new things and are achieving mastery over new tasks. Parents and teachers are very important during this stage. As parents, our codependency and perfectionism may get in the way of us allowing our child to go out and try new things. We may try to show them "the right way things are done" or stop them because "we are concerned they will get hurt," which can take a toll on the self-esteem of the child, who is trying to achieve a sense of initiative. If a child can do this, they will begin to feel a sense of confidence. Overly controlling parents may unfortunately begin to instill a sense of guilt in their child by not trusting them and sending the message *I don't think you're capable of doing this well.* Critical parents may unknowingly harp on what their child doesn't do right rather than the effort they put into the attempt. We want to really encourage our child during this time, praising them for putting in effort, not just for winning.

Industry vs. Inferiority is the crisis in the next stage in Erikson's model. This comprises children from ages five to thirteen. This stage of life is when society, teachers, coaches, and friends start to have a big impact. Children who do not measure up to societal norms may leave this stage deeply wounded. Even those who fit into many systemic norms may struggle. One way this time can be wounding is the vast amount of competition and comparison that goes on during this stage. Something as simple as how we grade children in school can be very negative for them. The grading system tends to be more focused on comparison to other children rather than a more subjective view of each individual child. In the current system, our children are pushed to be better than those around them, and when they don't measure up, it can be demoralizing. And our child is trying to navigate all this while trying also to fit in with their peers. This is the stage where you begin to see children turn to high-risk behaviors when they are struggling to adapt or fit in.

The hope is that you've been paying a lot of attention before we get to the next stage, the time of Identity vs. Role Confusion, which hits at adolescence, or the ages thirteen to twenty-one.

The adolescent stage of life has actually expanded in recent years and the term *extended adolescence* now applies to young adults in their early twenties. This stage is all about identifying who we are. A successful navigation of this phase is expected to result in a strong sense of self. Along the way, we may try on different roles, friends, or activities to learn who we are. Help your child explore these different phases. Don't get too caught up in any one identity but allow them to explore.

Unfortunately, if an adolescent really struggles in this phase, they may spend a large part of their twenties (and beyond) trying to figure out who they are, potentially extending their adolescence. Although we all continue to develop and evolve as our lives go on, if adolescents spend their teenage years rebelling or acquiescing, they are likely to spend their next stage continuing to behave more immaturely. Children from perfectionist households may begin to really fail during this time if they feel like they can't live up to the standards set out for them. They become apathetic twentysomethings who struggle to find the right job or anything motivating in their life.

In the next stage, Intimacy vs. Isolation (occurring between the ages of twenty-one and thirty-nine), we are working on forming our relationships with others. In this stage, you'll often see people struggling to have successful relationships with others because they are reenacting past trauma. You'll see adults act out their pain with partners and friends, keeping their distance if they have intimacy issues, a common result of perfectionist and codependent parenting. People will only truly thrive in this phase if they can heal the traumas of their past. Sadly, some people find themselves alone during this stage, unable to form meaningful relationships because the early trauma is so impactful.

Erikson's stages give us a snapshot of the importance of early development and how it plays into later years. As parents, it's our job to help our children navigate each of these psychosocial developmental stages so we can set them up for success as adults. Without understanding what a child may need to overcome, we may have a difficult time supporting them through it. It's important to educate ourselves on where our kids are at any given time.

NOW WHAT?

While reading this, you may have noticed where some of your own wounds have come from. If so, that's great! No need to be discouraged, since healing can happen at any point in life. This reminds me of one of my first and most impactful clients, a divorced man in his sixties who was fired from his finance job for showing up drunk. At the age of sixty-one, he not only got clean and sober from alcohol, but he also found a partner who helped him feel loved and alive again. He changed his career and became a substance abuse counselor as well! This illustrates the amazing changes we can make at any time. In my experience, it's never the amount of trauma but how willing you are to work on it. If you're ready to do the work, I suggest finding a therapist who specializes in a psychodynamic framework so that you can learn how your past informs your present and how you can go about healing.

REFLECTIVE EXERCISE

Identify the stage your child is in right now. What's the overarching crisis of this stage? List five ways you may be hindering them from accomplishing this stage and five ways you could help them successfully navigate this time of life.

CHAPTER 10

POSITIVE REINFORCEMENT

There's a saying that goes *What we focus on expands.* I love this idea, especially as it pertains to parenting. When we focus on our children's negative behavior, it's more likely to increase, and the same is true when we focus on their positive behavior. What we often don't realize is that we tend to interact more with our children about the negative than the positive. Think about it: It's easy to call out behavior we don't like. But we may forget to regularly verbalize all of our children's traits that we love.

When our children are accustomed to hearing more negative than positive from us, they will likely gravitate toward the negative. Unconsciously, they begin to believe that they can connect with us and get more attention when they are acting out. This creates a cycle of negative reinforcement (a focus on the "bad"). If you can shift your view of negative behavior as a cry for attention and begin instead to reinforce your child's positive behavior, you have a great opportunity to prevent this dynamic. One way I changed this in my family was by creating a "kindness chart." This positively reinforces our children for treating others well and behaving in positive ways. As much as possible, I focus on acknowledging positive behavior rather than "correcting" negative behavior.

This concept carries into all my relationships. When I'm not happy with someone, it's easy for me to pick apart all the things I don't like about them. I can become very righteous in my perception that they're doing things wrong—how dare they tell me something uncomplimentary about myself! I notice that when I'm more engaged in a negative perspective with someone, I can't help but get stuck in seeing only, or primarily, their negative qualities. I also notice that our relationship never seems to improve from this place. However, I've discovered that the reverse happens when I focus on the positive things about the other person. Be aware of how you may be unconsciously connecting with others in your life in a negative way, especially your children and spouse or partner.

We want our children to know what they have to offer, how deserving they are, and how wonderful they are. This leads to self-esteem, which we know is the surest guard against falling into perfectionist and codependent patterns. It's our job as parents to help our children feel good about themselves by building them up with positive reinforcement.

ACTIVITY

Carve out at least a half hour several times a week where you can just focus on your child individually. Let

> your child choose the activity, and leave all phones and devices at home. This is time for just you and your child to connect. Praise your child for acting in ways that are loving, kind, or empathic. Help them see the wonderful things about themselves.

A WARNING ABOUT ACCOMPLISHMENTS

When we focus our positive attention on our child's accomplishments (as opposed to their character), we unknowingly prime them to focus on accomplishments too. This creates perfectionist children. This approach feeds the ego, not the soul, and can lead a child to grow into an adult who cares more about doing things well or right than connecting with themselves, other people, their jobs, or any aspect of life on a deeper level. Many of these children become adults who end up in jobs that are "successful" but leave them unfulfilled. In my practice, I often work with adults who feel disconnected from themselves and their passions, and I must help them rediscover their true inner self—the one that's not linked to accomplishments but is just craving to connect with the world in a meaningful way.

When we focus too heavily on accomplishments, we teach our children to feed their confidence with temporary wins, rather than build their self-esteem from the inside out. To nourish your child's soul instead of their ego means we also need to let go of our own ego and stop getting stuck in how good it feels to see our child doing something well: winning their match, being chosen for a play, or getting good grades. Our attention must go deeper.

Give your kids beautiful feedback on who they are, not what they do. Get to know your child and see what lights them up. What do they get excited talking about? When do you see them smile? My parent clients tend to get so caught up in making sure their children are achieving that they don't focus on making sure their children are actually OK. Help guide them through their life, rather than making sure they get an A. It is much more useful to know how to cope with disappointment than it is to know all the presidents in order!

I recently had a pivotal session with a client, a woman in her late twenties who struggles with anxiety and creating intimate long-term relationships. In our work together, we discovered that she was deeply affected by her upbringing, which included pressure to play the piano professionally. She wasn't connected with piano and instead wanted to be in theater, but her parents didn't like that idea. The upper-class culture in which she grew up was focused on achieving, being the best, fitting in, and obtaining financial gain. Her desire to be a fun-loving drama girl wasn't aligned with her parents' expectations for her to be the best piano player in town. She even endured some abusive teaching throughout her time in music lessons, which only further impacted her in an activity she had no interest in doing. She ended up having to choose between herself and the positive reinforcement she was getting for something she didn't love. This left her with a lot of anxiety as an adult. Our work focused on bringing her back to who she really was.

REFLECTIVE EXERCISE

Can you identify resistance to an activity you're facing with your child? Perhaps they don't want to do gymnastics, or they want to quit playing the piano. Why is this activity important for you? Is it for them, or about you? It may be about you if:

- It's more difficult to get them to do it than it should be.
- They complain about it often.
- It would be embarrassing for you if they stopped.
- It will help them get into the best college.

It may be about them if:

- They really like the activity but have a hard time getting motivated.
- They often quit things, and you think it's important that they learn how to stick some things out.

If it's about you, I challenge you to let it go. If it's about them, sit down with your child and ask them how you can support them as they navigate what they're struggling with.

CHAPTER 11

ROLE MODELING

When it comes to parenting, there's nothing more important than *who you are*. Our kids learn the most from the behavior we model. As a codependent perfectionist, I knew I had a lot of work to do if I wanted to avoid instilling these same issues in my kids. It's up to us to break harmful generational patterns. You want to be a parent whose words and behaviors are in alignment. As my mentor once told me, "The best way to get someone to change is by showing it to them." So, although we can't directly change someone (codependency), when we work on ourselves (doing it for us, not them), we actually model good habits for our children, which will allow them to grow authentically.

So, now I challenge you with these questions: Who are you? Are you who you want your children to be? If these two things are in complete alignment, great! Skip to the next chapter! If not, this is your time for some self-reflection. What do you currently do that you do not wish your children to repeat? What do you want for them that you haven't prioritized for yourself? Think back to your vision for your child. Are you living it for yourself?

When your words and behaviors are in alignment, you can be a highly effective role model for your children. This is what we call Walking the Talk. As a therapist, I walk my talk. I do not preach to my clients. Instead, I lead my clients by example, which means that I've had to acknowledge and work on my many shortcomings. As Sophia Bush puts it, "You are allowed to be both a masterpiece and a work in progress, simultaneously." I like to role-model this for my clients and my children—it's the perfect mix of being self-loving and self-reflective.

As humans, we will always have things we need to work on. We will never be perfect beings. We are all gloriously imperfect! However, we need to own our imperfections and shortcomings. When one of your flaws comes to the surface, the greatest thing you can say to your child (or anyone) is, "I'm sorry." This is role modeling at its finest. We need to take responsibility for our behavior. We all get angry and sometimes say or do something we may later regret. Owning it can teach your child not only to do the same, but also to respect you. They will see you taking ownership over yourself and your behaviors. They will see you being human.

THE POWER OF APOLOGY

The other day I had a lovely conversation with a client who was struggling with parenting her teenagers. She told me how her daughter had begun sharing some thoughts about New Age hipsters and what she thought about them. My client acknowledged to me that she had quickly cut her daughter off and begun talking about her own perspective on the subject. Her daughter immediately shut down and said, "Never mind." The mom felt terrible. But she didn't know what to do. They had moved on, and it was now several days later. I expressed to her that it would be wonderful if she could go back to her daughter and take responsibility for talking over her and preventing her daughter from sharing her own perspective.

We often underestimate the impact that ownership of our behavior has on our children. It really shows them we understand our faults and have self-compassion. This is a great lesson for them! It's also important for them to learn that it's OK to say, "I'm sorry." It's not enough to simply tell our children that they need to apologize when they do something wrong or hurt someone's feelings. We have to model this by actually doing it ourselves, even when it's uncomfortable. If you tell your children it's important to apologize if they've done something wrong, but then you never apologize to them, you are teaching them something else entirely: not to trust you.

Many of my clients have lamented that their parents have never apologized to them. Many parents seem to think that apologizing is a sign of weakness. But it is actually a great strength. There is bravery in being fallible. I love when I hear a parent apologizing to their child. It's such a beautiful acknowledgment of being human, and it means so much to the kid.

TEACH BY EXAMPLE

Consistency between your behavior and speech is also important. Be aware of this in your everyday life. Do you do what you say is important? For example, if you tell your children they shouldn't make fun of people because it's not nice, do you also follow that advice? Or do they catch you being judgmental of someone else?

As M. Scott Peck states, "If a child sees his parents day in and day out behaving with self-discipline, restraint, dignity, and a capacity to order their own lives, then the child will come to feel in the deepest fibers of his being that this is the way to live" (*The Road Less Traveled*, p. 21). Who we are is the biggest lesson our children will learn. We teach by example, good or bad!

Role-modeling self-acceptance is also crucial. If you want your child to accept all of themselves, then you must show them what that looks like.

> Kevin, a twenty-nine-year-old male, lamented over how bad he was for not doing his taxes for the past three years. Is this a problem? Sure. This client beat himself up daily for this and his many other self-destructive behaviors. Kevin also came from a father with a gambling addiction that he never acknowledged. Kevin saw his father not care about himself and be destructive with money. It's not surprising that Kevin was also gambling on his future and had a distorted relationship with money. Kevin's parents judged him for his issues and also gave him extra money to try to help him get out of debt.
>
> Not only were Kevin's parents enabling him, but they were clearly unaware of their own dysfunction and were instead focused on Kevin. What they didn't realize was that their own behavior had a strong impact on Kevin's relationship with money, self-care, and responsibility. Everyone in this family would benefit from acknowledging their own issues and teaching others by taking responsibility for their actions.
>
> Jasmine, a thirty-year-old woman, came in for therapy reporting to me that she was lazy and unmotivated

and needed to change. She asked if I could help her become more disciplined and shared with me all her destructive behaviors. Session after session, she went on and on about the ways she was lazy and unmotivated, such as not working hard for her entire workday or not doing her laundry regularly. Sometimes she even took shortcuts in her life like ordering takeout a couple times a week. (Gasp!) This same "lazy" woman was also a college graduate with a successful job, living on her own in a different city from her family, paying her own bills, and had many friends. She was actually far from lazy and unmotivated, but this was the story her parents had told her as they modeled it to her through similar behaviors. Both mechanical engineers, they taught Jasmine that if they weren't consistently on top of everything and always busy, then they were simply lazy. It was my job to help her see the story she had developed about herself because of her parents' perspectives and question if it was really true. She was a true perfectionist and had limited empathy for herself, just as her parents had had for themselves. In this case, the problem wasn't her behavior; the problem was her learned perspective of her behavior.

Help your children accept themselves by genuinely accepting *yourself*—not just pushing them to be different. This breaks the pattern of perfectionism.

YOUR ANXIETY CAN BECOME YOUR CHILD'S ANXIETY

According to *Counseling Individuals Through the Lifespan* (Wong, Hall, Justice, Hernandez): "Anxiety disorders are the most common form of psychopathology in children." It's possible that this is related to parents using fear as a form of behavior modification and feeling the pressure from a perfectionist parent. In my experience, it's also highly connected with the parent's level of anxiety. It's important to understand that, when it comes to your child, your anxiety becomes their anxiety.

Anxiety is common among parents. This is understandable—parenting can be stressful! It's easy to feel a lot of anxiety about the many things outside of our control that can happen to our children. Unfortunately, when we feel out of control, it's common to try to control more. I often see parents who are unknowingly creating a lot of anxiety in their children by exposing them to their own anxieties. For instance, I meet many parents who would "never trust a stranger" to watch their children. I understand how difficult it can be to trust other people, but by never allowing your children space from you, or never allowing outside people to become trusted people in their life, you're teaching your children to be scared of the world. You want your child to actually learn to discern the difference between a stranger who feels trustworthy and one who doesn't, and how to learn to trust appropriately.

We don't want our children to feel too timid to explore because life is dangerous. We want to protect them, but we don't want to overdo it just because they might scrape their knees. Let them fall. Let them get to know the world around them, build resilience, and set their own boundaries. Be mindful about looking at what scares you and how this may impact your child. In my podcast, *The Codependent Perfectionist*, I discuss a parent who wouldn't let her son play soccer because of her own fears about him getting hurt. This is very different from really trying to save someone from danger. This instills unnecessary fear in the child.

As perfectionists and codependents, we can also have anxieties about many things beyond our children's safety, such as how they do or do not fit in with others, how people see and experience our children, whether people are in judgment of their having dyed hair or a tattoo, or whether our children are good at sports, dance, or any other activity. It's important that we realize that this is our stuff. If we had similar issues as children, we can be especially anxious about what our children may go through when they're different or not as good as others in these areas.

If you yourself have been diagnosed with a serious mental health issue such as anxiety, your child is likely to have that same issue. What's most important is not that you beat yourself up for whatever it is that you struggle with, but that you show your child what it looks like to cope effectively. Go to therapy, get support, work on it, talk about it. When we get swallowed alive by our mental health issues and don't take care of ourselves, we teach our children to do the same. If we get the help we need, we can become the best parents for our kids, ensure that they don't take on our issues, and model how to find help and support when needed. Your fear will only create anxiety in your child. It's your job to work on it!

> **REFLECTIVE EXERCISE**

What makes you anxious as a parent? Make a list. Be open and honest with yourself. Try to identify how this may be impacting your child. If you are open to it, create a spiritual practice speaking to your higher power about all your anxieties. Ask your higher power for support and guidance. Reflect on three ways you can work on your own anxiety so you don't pass it on to your children.

CHAPTER 12

BREAK THE CYCLE

"You cannot change what you aren't aware of."
— Deepak Chopra

In my practice, I begin every new client intake session the same way: with a genogram. Genograms are simply psychological family trees, mapping out a client's history in terms of dynamics, patterns, and cycles spanning generations.

With a simple genogram, I can identify much of the function and dysfunction going on in any given family, as well as the many strengths and resiliencies a client may unknowingly possess. Dysfunction occurs in family patterns—it's literally passed down through a mix of genetics and behavioral teachings. Some of the patterns in a family may include people who are hardworking, active politically, nature-loving, or involved in functional marriages, as well as things like addiction, abuse, codependency, perfectionism, divorce, and mental illness.

Let's take a look at this sample genogram I created for a client of mine after asking about their family history. It might seem complicated at first, but this is really just some of the basics. You'll notice some information about cultural background, generational status, and religion. You'll also see that there's some potentially negative family patterns like divorce, alcoholism, codependency (COD), favoritism, and strained relationships. You'll also notice some resiliencies and positive traits like sobriety, career expertise, successful marriages, and supportive relationships. This tells me a lot about the patterns that we're working with and how we may need to go about healing the cycles.

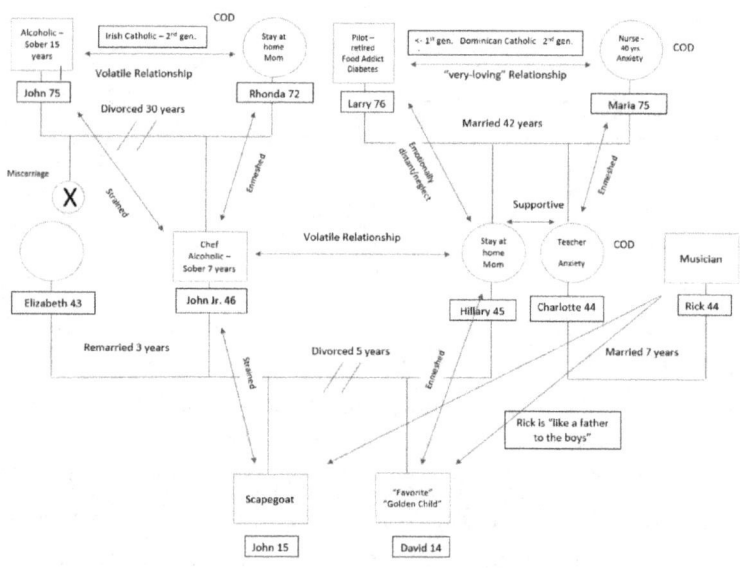

Freedom can come when we recognize that although we may be primed toward certain behaviors because of our genetics (in the case of addiction) or learned behaviors (in the case of being in an emotionally abusive relationship), we also have the ability to work with these predispositions. For example, if we know we are predisposed to addiction, we can take preventative measures in our own behavior and in how we parent our children. We may choose to explain this predisposition and share the family history with our children (at the appropriate age, of course) so they have an understanding of the stakes when the choice to use drugs or alcohol presents itself during adolescence and beyond.

Or, if we are predisposed to be in emotionally abusive relationships, we can seek support like therapy to help us strengthen ourselves so we don't accept abuse from others. It's important as parents that we work on showing our children what a balanced relationship looks like so that they will be predisposed to that instead, effectively breaking the pattern. In another example, if we had a father who didn't know how to express anger without flying off the handle, it's likely that we either repress our own anger or have similar outbursts. It's helpful for us to learn the skills of expressing anger effectively so that we can pass them on to our children.

Thankfully, humans are resilient and capable of change! Although many harmful family patterns are based on a combination of environmental and genetic factors, we are in no way doomed to recreate or be stuck with these patterns, and neither are our children. And we want our children to know that. As children, we don't have the ability to decide what is passed down to us. As young adults, however, we can make better choices based on the knowledge of these patterns and eventually model a new way for our own children.

Stopping a family cycle is some of the hardest work you might ever do; however, it gives you and your child the opportunity to live a more fulfilling life. I can't think of anything more beautiful than that.

REFLECTIVE EXERCISE

Do your own genogram! Use the key below to help you.

Fill in yourself and your children. Fill in your partner, your parents, and your partner's parents. Add siblings, with younger to the right and older to the left. Add in ages. Identify any addictive behaviors for each person. Identify relationship patterns (people who are estranged, who left others, who are divorced, etc.), and mark an *X* for anyone who has passed away and note how they died. Name any medical conditions. Identify any mental health conditions and substance abuse issues, and indicate those who have received treatment or are sober.

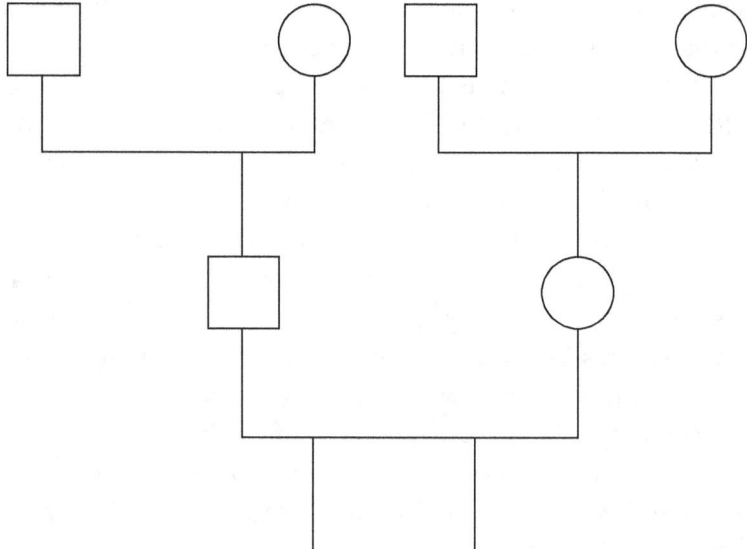

Note the length of relationships. Here are some basic symbols you can use to create your genogram, as well as a blank genogram to be filled in. This includes symbols for a family headed by a heterosexual couple, but feel free to alter the symbols as appropriate for your own family!

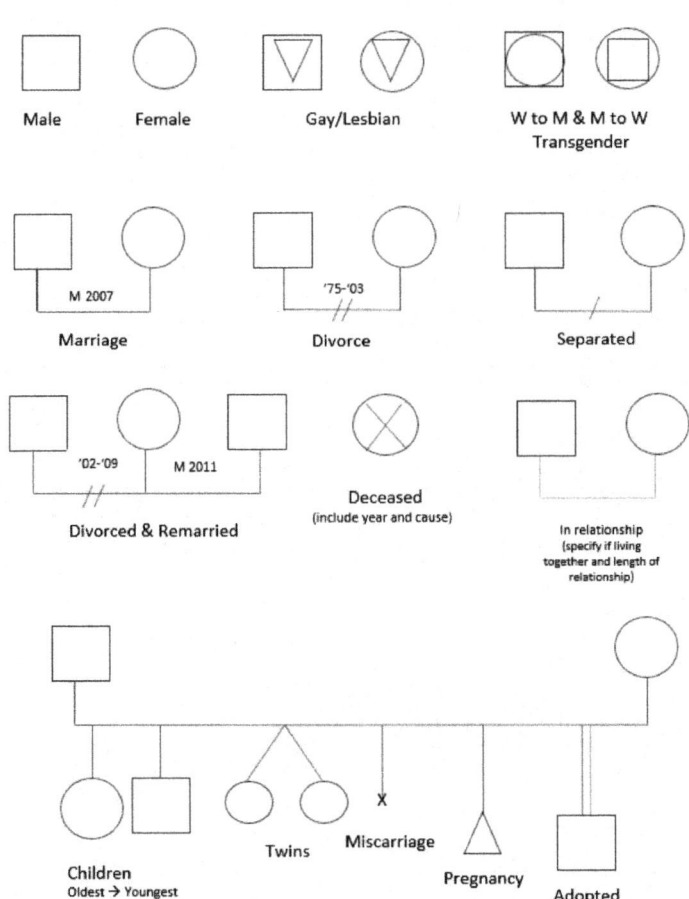

CHAPTER 13

CLARITY & COMMUNICATION

Clear communication is crucial in any relationship. It allows others to understand your behavior and, most importantly, the intentions behind your behavior. We earn the trust of others when our behavior and our words are in alignment.

Consider the last time someone said something to you that left you confused about what they meant. For example, let's say you're talking to your sister on the phone about speaking up to your child's principal about something you didn't agree with, and your sister remarks, "Of course you would do that!" This could mean so many things. If this simple statement isn't explained further, you might come up with your own negative meaning behind the statement, such as *My sister always makes fun of me when I do something I think is right.* But this explanation isn't based on fact—it's only a story in your head. The best thing to do is to ask for clarification of comments before you make assumptions that might cause further tension in the relationship.

Another way a lack of clarity can be damaging is when we project our experience from our past trauma onto the present moment. For example, if we had highly critical parents, we may hear simple statements as harsh or critical even when they are completely neutral. I remember my mentor giving me a directive during a training, something as simple as, "No, don't do that." There was no emphasis in her voice when she said this, but I heard it as a harsh *Don't do that!* I even said to a peer, "Oh, Stephanie just yelled at me not to do that." My mentor turned around and said, "You know, Alana, I didn't yell at you." And she was right. She didn't! But it was hard for me to even hear a directive without feeling like someone was yelling at me. We filter our life experiences through the stories we already have in our heads. This type of projection can also bring a lack of clarity to our communication.

To avoid putting damaging storylines in our children's heads, the best thing to do is to be as clear about our reasons and intentions as we can. This way our children won't unintentionally begin to make up meanings about our behavior and words. For instance, if we don't allow them to go off with their friends where we can't see them and we don't explain *why*, the child may interpret that as *I'm not safe*, rather than *This particular situation isn't safe*. I regularly walk my children through my thoughts and reasons for this exact reason.

The writer Elizabeth Gilbert once gave a great example of what happens when parents aren't clear about their actions in her article in O magazine called "The One Skill That Helps You Live a Happier Life." She shared the story of her father and his two adult siblings getting together after their mother died. One sibling shared how they loved how their mother always tested the milk before she gave it to them to make sure it wasn't spoiled. Then another sibling chimed in and said, "That's not why she drank the milk before she gave it to us! It was because she overfilled the glass!" and the third sibling said, "You're both wrong! She was stealing our damn milk!" Her point was that all three children had completely different views of the exact same behavior by their mother. It's very likely the mother assumed that her children knew exactly why she was doing what she was doing. But they didn't! They each filled in their own explanation. Children need clarity from their parents from everything as small as tasting milk to larger lessons. Something as small as saying, *Ah, the milk is still fresh, now you can have some* makes a big change in their experience.

LANGUAGE

My clients are most likely sick of me stressing the importance of language, but I can't emphasize it enough. Language is impactful, and we always want to choose our words wisely. The good old saying, *Sticks and stones will break my bones, but words will never hurt me* could not be more wrong. In real life, we are far more harmed by words than by sticks and stones! It's the words that really stay with us. Words translate to thoughts, which translate to emotions. As a therapist, I consistently look at the language my clients are using. It reveals so much about what they feel and believe about themselves, other people, and the world.

In one of my therapeutic groups, one parent once recounted how he often yelled at his children because he couldn't contain his own rage, anger, and frustration. He recognized that he had issues with anger but also wasn't yet ready to release this. Codependency came in with his wife, who acted as a caretaker of him and his feelings. After he yelled at the children, she would say to them, "You know, he's yelling at you because he loves you." This is not only incorrect and unclear, but it also leaves the children with the message that it's OK for the father to yell at them because it's out of love. But he's not yelling out of love! It's out of frustration and because he is not dealing with his own issues. A much more honest and effective statement from the mother would be, *He is struggling. He has a hard time not yelling when he gets frustrated. It's not your fault, and he loves you, but he needs to learn how to express himself differently with us. This isn't OK.* See the difference here? I'm not suggesting that it needs to be an extreme change, like a divorce, or even that the father can't get angry, but instead that we need to be clear that our feelings are not our children's fault or responsibility. That starts with language.

Another issue with language is when we label. Labeling is a common societal practice. It actually helps our mind make sense of things and not have to think so hard. All children will do things like tell a lie, cry, fuss, or throw a tantrum. These behaviors are universal and totally normal. But all too often, parents and families make them *mean something* about the person. *Tamara is sensitive. John is a hard ass. Brian is hyper.* These types of labels infiltrate a person's self-perception from a young age and can become self-fulfilling prophecies. Positive labels such as *Tasha is so sweet* or *Derek is strong* can be damaging, too. These labels can also be damaging because they are limiting and put our child into a box where they may have trouble seeing themselves differently. What about when Derek struggles or when Tasha is mean? Children really internalize the labels we create for them.

Another example of labeling occurs in situations such as when someone breaks the law and we call them a criminal. Yes, a criminal is someone who has broken the law. However, we often don't consider the impact that such a label has on someone. It implies that they are different from us, as if we aren't capable of that same behavior. Years ago I talked to a corrections officer about how he navigated the system so well. He told me that he lived by the notion that he was just one decision away from being an inmate at any time. He didn't see himself as above them. He saw himself as just having chosen a different path, one not at all far from their path. By doing this, he removed the stigma from those in the penal system, treating them as equals, with respect and empathy.

His words have stuck with me. We are all just one moment away from being in a much different position. This mindset can apply to addiction, abuse, incarceration, disability, and many other things. Our society doesn't like to acknowledge this. We like to label people and treat them as "other." We lean into black-and-white thinking. We have a hard time looking at and acknowledging the complexities in life in ourselves, and especially in others. But the truth is that just because we act in a certain way, or make a poor decision, doesn't mean we're bad people. We want to help our children understand these complexities and never judge who they are from one decision or action, good or bad. Using language with care and avoiding labels can be really helpful in communicating this.

If my child tells a lie and I call them a liar, I've just labeled them. The child then internalizes this as part of who they are, instead of understanding it as a negative behavior with consequences. There is nothing wrong with identifying the truth, that the child has lied. However, if we turn it into a concrete idea about who the child *is*, it becomes problematic. Be careful to distinguish between *You are* and *You did*.

Guilt and shame are significantly connected with this type of language. When we experience guilt, we believe we've done something wrong. When we experience shame, we believe there is *something wrong with us*. We never want our children to feel shame about who they are. A little guilt is OK—it can teach someone to try to do better next time. But shame is highly connected with perfectionist behavior. The person, feeling ashamed of themselves, will often turn to perfectionism to mask who they are. They try to earn love with their perfectness instead.

Our language can be really damaging when we aren't careful about it. Like when we tell a child something "isn't a big deal" when it is to them, or when we say they should "just get over it." I can't tell you how many clients I've seen who have told me something *isn't a big deal* that is actually horrendous, even smiling at me when talking about abuse they've experienced. When children feel that their feelings are wrong, based on what they hear from the adults around them, they are likely to begin to believe that there's something wrong with them for feeling a particular way.

We also need to be careful never to leave our child feeling less loved after they engage in an activity that we don't agree with. This can be really tough. Language comes in strongly here. We want our children to know when we don't agree with something. But we also want them to know that what they do doesn't affect how much we love them. Try to help your child explore how and why they made a decision. Share similar stories from your own life. Give yourself time to feel when you're upset with your children. Then, when you are calm and rational, sit down and talk, encouraging the child to express themselves and reminding them that you love them no matter what.

THE INNER CRITIC

We all think critically about ourselves at times. However, some of us have very harsh inner critics that impact how we feel about ourselves on a daily basis. The inner critic is also highly correlated with shame (the belief that there is something wrong with us). Sadly, this inner critic is usually unnecessarily mean and finds ways to turn innocuous experiences into evidence about how we are not good enough.

The inner critic is a voice that is formed from our childhood experiences. It is strongly tied to our parents and other authority figures, specifically the language they've used to describe us. Statements such as *You're clumsy*, *You're stupid*, and *You don't think* become ingrained in us, and we begin to repeat them to ourselves as we grow up. It's someone else's (possibly multiple people's) voice that at some point in life became our own voice in our head. In especially harsh environments, a person will typically form a very active and powerful inner critic. This can also happen in environments where language is simply not considered thoughtfully. The inner critic is likely to be a voice that labels our behavior with judgment. It is not compassionate or understanding of why we may have made a bad choice or the circumstances of why something happened. It often blames and finds fault with who we are and how we act, sometimes even when our behavior is perfectly OK.

This makes me think of many of my clients, but one in particular who had a Godzilla-like inner critic.

> Luke was born into a middle-class immigrant family. They came to America for more opportunity and lived a comfortable lifestyle, but they were hyperfocused on Luke's future and on him being "successful." From what Luke remembers, he spent much of his childhood alone, and when his parents were around, they tended to fixate on his grades and extracurricular activities. At age forty-five, Luke came to see me after losing his job and a long-term relationship. He revealed that he had never been content with life. He went to a college picked out by his mother, went into a career that his father said was safe and good, and had rarely felt in control of his own path. Not only was he discontented with life, but his inner critic was sabotaging his every

move. Whenever he didn't do something he was "supposed to do," he would revert into his childhood self and tell himself how "bad" he was. Every time he considered doing something that could potentially make him happy, he would question it and back away. He would also berate himself for not pursuing what he wanted. Luke was more interested in making sure the people around him were happy, because he believed everyone else was more important than him (as his inner critic often reminded him). Until he could separate from his inner critic and take the risks necessary to care for himself, Luke would be unable to find peace and joy in his life. What he needed to learn was how to recognize that the inner voice was not his, but that of his parents. It was cruel, harsh, unforgiving, and fearful.

Although Luke didn't come from a particularly cruel or physically abusive family, he came from a cold perfectionist family that used language in a way that created a negative framework in Luke's head about who he was. His parents cared more about him "making it" than they did about Luke's emotional health, which he could never quite manage. Ironically, the reason he couldn't make it was because of his inner critic, which began in his family and was at the heart of his lack of belief in himself! It's very important that we understand that a lack of emotional nurturing is quite possibly the most damaging of all types of abuse. It's up to us to show love, compassion, and concern for our children through not only our behavior but also how we speak to them, providing them with positive language about themselves so that they use this language rather than the negative inner critic's. We are partly, if not strongly, responsible for how our children see and speak to themselves.

REFLECTIVE EXERCISE

Let's find out about your inner critic! Write down a description of this voice in your head. What does it sounds like? What does it say? How often does it talk to you? Next, take the stories your inner critic tells about you and turn them into the opposite statement. For example, *I'm not smart enough* becomes *I'm more than smart enough!* Do this for all the negative stories that play on repeat in your mind. How do you feel?

Now think about your children. To start, identify five positive stories you can tell them about themselves, about all their efforts, strength, and courage. Start a daily practice of using positive language with your children.

CHAPTER 14

HOLDING SPACE & LISTENING

Holding space is what I do as a therapist. It means that I drop my assumptions and desire to fix and instead provide a space for my clients to feel that I am holding them emotionally. This doesn't mean that I don't give advice when asked or at important times. But most of my time with my clients is NOT spent giving advice. Instead, I strongly believe that all my clients (and all people) have their own answers. My job is to help them uncover their answers within. We do this together on a therapeutic journey.

As humans, we connect most deeply with others when we drop our need to be heard and just listen. It's amazing how hard this can be and how accustomed we are to a more back-and-forth conversation around our thoughts and opinions rather than simply just trying to listen and understand. Experiment with this by being in conversation with someone and trying not to respond to what they're saying with advice or a similar experience. Your one and only goal is to listen and make sure you fully understand what the other person is saying. This is the essence of mirroring!

EMPOWERING WITH MIRRORING

Many parents feel it is their role to give advice when their children have questions, concerns, or difficulties. To that, I say, "Do the opposite. Fight the urge to give advice UNLESS they ask for it." We all tend to think we have the answers for everyone. If only they would ___, then they would be/feel ___. As much as we may believe we know what is right for our children (and maybe we do), we still need to take a step back and allow them to come up with their own solutions.

Mirroring is a beautiful technique that helps people hear and see themselves. In doing this, people start to process their own thoughts and emotions and get closer to their true selves, which is where the answers lie. This builds self-esteem. It also gives the child the necessary space they need so they don't feel like we are meddling with their issues (in the case of codependency). Instead of giving advice, utilize mirroring.

Here's an example of your average non-connecting conversation between a parent and a child:

> John: I'm thinking about dropping swim team and only doing baseball.
> Mom: You can't drop swim—only quitters give up! And think of all the time and effort you've put in. It would be such a waste for you to stop after all this time.

John: But it's too much! I don't like waking up that early! I'm not doing it!

Mom: But think about how the team will feel. You've been with them for so many years. You're one of their star swimmers.

In this dialogue, there is no connection. In fact, both parties may leave the conversation feeling dissatisfied and even frustrated. John leaves feeling unheard and guilty about wanting to leave the team and doesn't like being labeled a quitter. He's frustrated that his mom doesn't understand why he doesn't want to be on the team anymore. Mom might feel disappointed that he wants to stop swimming after all the time and energy they've both devoted over the years. Plus, it looks bad to have him leave the team, which may be bringing up her own codependent and perfectionist issues.

Now here's the same conversation done with mirroring:

John: I'm thinking about dropping swim team and only doing baseball.

Mom: So, you're thinking about dropping swim team and only doing baseball?

John: Yes, I'm having a hard time balancing everything. It's exhausting to wake up early and then stay late for baseball. I barely have any time to get my homework done or see friends.

Mom: So, you want to drop swimming because it's getting in the way of you balancing everything. You're exhausted from waking up early and then staying late for baseball. You're having a tough time getting your homework done and seeing friends. Did I get that right?

John: Yeah, exactly. I've thought about it a lot, and I actually enjoy baseball a lot more, so I'd rather focus on that and spend the extra time I have getting back on track with school and seeing my friends more often.

Mom: OK, I think I got it. You realized that you actually enjoy baseball more, and you'd rather spend your time focusing on school and friends than waking up early to practice for swim?

John: Yep.

Mom: OK, it sounds like you've put a lot of thought into that decision. Let me know how I can best support you with this. If you want any feedback from me, I'd be happy to share my thoughts. I do have some concerns about you letting go of swimming that I'd like to share with you if you're open to hearing them.

Mirroring can be difficult for many parents at first because it pushes you to hold back from going to advice-giving. I get it. As parents, we always want to share our thoughts! Many parents would find this type of communication ridiculous, because they believe their role is to tell their children the right way to live. However, mirroring goes along with that favorite adage of mine: *Give a man a fish, feed him for a day. Teach a man to fish, feed him for a lifetime.*

Mirroring in conversation is much more adultlike. It teaches your child that you're a safe person to share with. It also helps you move toward a framework that allows your child to make decisions and learn from them. When we mirror, we are holding space. We are truly listening to our children, not just hearing their words. When we listen, we allow for deeper connection. Remember, your children are their own people, not simply extensions of you. As their parent, you are not here to shape them into the person you want them to be. You are here to allow them to blossom into the person they are meant to be.

REFLECTIVE EXERCISE

Put mirroring into practice!

Use the example above for reference. Next time you speak with your child, make sure to only respond by repeating back to them what you heard them say. Try to phrase it as a question. For example, "So, you're upset with your best friend because she didn't call you back?" When you're not sure of exactly what they said, ask them for clarity. Do not interpret what they say or fill in any blanks with your own words. Only use their words! Once you get to a *yes* response, it means you mirrored well! Then you can ask your own questions or make your own statements. Try not to make your questions or comments intrusive, such as *Don't you think you should . . . ?* or *I think it's silly you're feeling that way.* Just let your child share with you, listen, and mirror. Watch the magic take place.

Here's another simple example to guide you:

You: How was your day, honey?
Child: Fine. Nothing special. We watched a movie in history class today.
You: Ah, so your day was fine? Nothing special happened, and you watched a movie in history class?
Child: Yep!
You: Nice, could you tell me more about the movie?

CHAPTER 15

ALLOWING FOR *ALL* EMOTIONS

No emotions are inherently good or bad. Let me say that again: *No emotions are good or bad.* Emotions simply ARE. Many of us have become culturally conditioned to think we should not experience anger, frustration, sadness, or any other "negative" feeling because that means there's something wrong with us. Perhaps we were taught that these are bad emotions, and we need to get rid of them. Unfortunately, that's simply not true—and it's not possible! All humans are built to have all kinds of feelings. We need to be very mindful about not teaching our children to only have a small range of feelings that we find to be more pleasant. Even anger can be an important feeling that helps show our children when they are not OK with something.

I see many adults who were programmed not to feel certain feelings. Unfortunately, if we grow up in a home that does not fully honor our emotional experience, we may have a very difficult time functioning as an adult. I often see people who are struggling with relationships or life in general as a result of limited emotional discourse in their childhoods. This is called emotional neglect. When a family doesn't discuss, address, or attend to emotions, it can be harmful for children. They learn not to value their feelings, and as a result they have no language to identify, experience, or explore them. This tends to create adults who are functional in many external ways yet feel depressed and anxious and who face great challenges in relationships.

As codependents, it can be very hard to sit with a child in their feelings, especially when the feelings are intense. Take a look at how you hold space for your child when they have feelings. Does it bring up discomfort in you? Do you try to change your child's feelings as soon as possible? Do you get angry with them for having negative feelings? Remember, substance abuse is highly connected with a person's inability to sit with their own feelings. Work on trying to hold better space for your children to avoid more serious issues later on.

Our own cultural conditioning can also get in the way here. For example, we try to get boys not to experience or express sadness because we're taught this makes them "less of a man." We have a hard time allowing girls to be angry, as this is seen as unacceptable behavior for a girl. Be mindful of your own underlying conditioned perspectives. When people have been taught not to feel, their feelings remain stuck somewhere in their body. They become detached from these feelings, and then they often come out in other ways that are more concerning. A big one is anger turned inward, which can manifest as self-hatred, depression, or perfectionism and can lead to more serious problems, such as addiction to numb the unpleasant feelings.

When our children are screaming, crying, or doing other distressing things, we will likely feel the urge to make them stop. I have that urge myself! Many of you may say, "Well, of course, we're their parents and we care!" Yes, that may be true, but acting on that urge and trying to fix your child's feelings is actually problematic. We may not like many of the feelings our children have, but that's *our issue*, not our children's. For example, if my child gets angry and I react to it with anger, that's my issue! There's no inherent reason I should be angry over her anger, except that it's probably tapping into some of my own issues. Perhaps not having my own space to be angry as a child? Or my unrealistic expectations for my child and how she should behave? It's important to let our children experience all emotions and see them as a normal part of life. This helps them have compassion for themselves and others.

THERE ARE NO BAD EMOTIONS

In American society, we tend to label emotions such as anger, frustration, and sadness as bad emotions, and happiness, cheerfulness, and lightheartedness as good emotions. In our codependency, we try to get other people to feel the feelings we want them to feel; we don't like when they have bad feelings (because we tend to take them on and feel them ourselves). Unfortunately, when we do this as parents, we teach our children that they should rid themselves of negative feelings rather than learn how to be with these feelings.

Comforting our children as they experience their more difficult feelings is important, and it's even more important to teach our children how to comfort themselves. From an early age, I worked with my oldest daughter to teach her how to soothe herself when she got upset because she had very intense reactions to things. We have sat together many times as I've coached her on calming herself through breathing and hugging her stuffies, or when she was younger, using her pacifier. I would also ask her if she wanted or needed a hug or back rub, and sometimes she did, other times she didn't. All this can start as early as infancy! Teaching children to soothe themselves rather than changing their feelings. Comforting is not the same thing as fixing. Comfort away! Give your child hugs if they are open to it and always give love. Let them know you're there with them. Try to understand what they may be feeling and why. You don't need to agree with them or get it or tell them to feel something else. If you can learn to empathize with your child, without fixing them, you are well on your way to breaking codependent cycles and parenting with excellence!

A good example of this is my own experience growing up. I wasn't a happy, smiley child. I didn't walk around with a scowl on my face all the time; I just didn't smile often. I was shy and withdrawn. I was contending with depression from early on. I distinctly remember a woman at a department store turning to me and saying, "You should smile more!" In that moment, I felt even sadder. Instead of her trying to get to know or understand me in any way, she told me that what I was doing wasn't right and tried to change how I was feeling. I felt judged. It's small moments like this that can be highly impactful for a child. She was just another adult who didn't try to understand me but instead tried to change me.

Not surprisingly, I have a child who also doesn't smile all the time. It's hard for me because it brings up a lot of my own issues as a child, and I have to be careful not to enmesh into her and try to get her to change her emotional expression. Instead, it's actually my job to protect her from adults who have a reaction to her emotional expression because they don't like it. My job is to let her be and tell others to back off gently or kindly, so that they don't harm her with their own issues.

It's hard for us not to conceptualize emotions as positive or negative, but again we must try our best not to do so. The next time you see your child experiencing an emotion and you find yourself reacting to it, pause. Ask yourself, *What is this bringing up for me?* Also ask yourself, *How can I be there for my child right now without trying to change them?* Avoid statements that indicate your desire to get them out of their feelings in that moment.

A few days ago, one of my daughters started crying because her sister wouldn't give her a hug when she wanted it. Although the crying can be unpleasant, my response was, "I can understand why you're upset about your sister not wanting to give you a hug. She doesn't need to give you a hug if she doesn't want to, but you're allowed to be upset about it." In this teaching moment, I'm sharing with her that she should go ahead and feel upset if that's what's coming up for her, but it's not her sister's job to do something she doesn't want to just so she feels better. I'm also not going to change her emotional experience of this but just let her feel it.

NOT CHANGING EMOTIONS

Not only is it important not to label your child when they have feelings, you want to be very mindful about not trying to *change what they are feeling* (codependency). When we are showing love to someone, we accept all of who they are, not just "the good parts." In this way, we also accept all their emotions as a natural part of being human. When we show our children that we accept all their emotions, we help them learn to accept them as well, which ushers them toward wholeness rather than compartmentalization or suppression. Even when we see our children in distress, it is not our job to make them feel any different. It is our job to help them be with their feelings and eventually work through them.

One of the more damaging things said to me growing up was *What do you have to be upset about? You have everything.* What I heard was *You have no reason to feel the way you feel.* These people were trying to change my feelings. This type of response shuts a child down and prevents them from expressing themselves and being with their emotions.

When we grow up in homes where our emotions are not nurtured, we can develop very unhealthy coping mechanisms. This can lead to all sorts of mental health-related issues. When you become a parent, it's also extremely difficult to honor your child's range of emotions if you do not honor your own. If you have difficulty accepting any "negative" emotions, you may want to seek out a therapist to work through some of these difficulties so you don't continue the cycle.

HAVING A "SENSITIVE" CHILD

Never call your child "sensitive" or "too sensitive." Or "crybaby," or any other term that has the potential to make them feel like there's something wrong with them for simply expressing their emotions. When we call a child too sensitive, we're telling them that their emotional experience is wrong and that we are right.

I didn't say something hurtful. You are just too sensitive.

What's really going on is that we are not OK with their emotional experience and the idea that we might have hurt our child's feelings (codependency), and instead we tell them that there's something wrong with them. This is a defense against looking at ourselves. Labeling our children "sensitive" or "too sensitive" often gives them the idea that they are feeling too much, and they need to stop feeling so much because it's a burden on their parents and everyone else. Since people don't have control over their feelings, teaching them this idea is dysfunctional, damaging, and shame-inducing. I work with countless adults who were labeled sensitive children. Adults told them that they felt too much and needed to stop. We don't want our children not to feel feelings. This can prime someone toward substance abuse or other addictive issues, where they use a substance, activity, or person to push the feelings away.

If you notice that your child is more impacted by emotions than other children, your job is to parent them accordingly, instead of labeling them as sensitive. You want to help them cope with their emotional experiences. Many people who are empathic tend to pick up on others' energy or feelings very easily, becoming easily overwhelmed. They can sense many things and are highly impacted by the feelings around them. This can be a really helpful quality when channeled effectively because these children are very in touch with themselves and others. From an early age, I was very adept at feeling people's energy, which has helped me tremendously in my work and personal life. However, it was tough at times when others simply didn't understand me and thought I was just shy. Like me, these types of children can have a difficult time feeling understood as well as being in certain spaces and with certain people. Trust your child's instincts and encourage them to do the same. It's important for your child to learn to listen to their intuition.

Some common signs of empathic or intuitive children include:

- Picking up on other people's energies
- Seeing things we adults cannot see (such as colors, angels, or people)
- Showing psychic abilities
- Having difficulty in certain spaces or with certain people

- Being easily affected by certain sounds or touches (maybe even the clothes they wear)
- Asking highly insightful questions
- Having trouble with others being sad around them
- Having strong emotional reactions to things such as change, boundaries being implemented, and not getting their way
- Appearing highly intelligent for their age

Be careful about how you parent these children. If you tell them their thoughts or feelings are silly, you will be squelching their spirit. Don't laugh at them for what they say. These children often go underground with who they are and what they experience because they think there's something wrong with them based on the feedback they get from others. Find out more about what they are experiencing. It can actually be pretty fascinating! Most of these children know way more than we do. Learn from them.

The Indigo Children (1999) is a great resource for parents of empathic or sensitive children. It provides a solid understanding of children who are highly intuitive and specifically explores how to parent them effectively. As *The Indigo Children* and many other publications state, a lot of these children are inappropriately labeled as having mental health issues in today's modern society. We need to be very careful about this, as it can have lasting negative impact and even lead parents to medicate children who don't have a true mental illness. Many schools aren't well equipped to deal with highly empathic children, so you may need to consider a more supportive environment.

REFLECTIVE EXERCISE

Reflect and write about how you were parented. Sit and breathe and allow yourself to go back in time to recall one or more experiences of getting upset or angry as a child. What was it like for you? How did your parents handle it? How did they deal with their own "negative" emotions? Did you feel loved during these moments? Were you punished for feeling? Did your parents process their own feelings well? How did they work through their own emotions? All this will bring clarity about how you process and label feelings and what you may be passing on to your own children.

CHAPTER 16

HOW TO LOVE OUR KIDS

We have so many misconceptions about what love is. I prefer M. Scott Peck's description of love as not so much a feeling as an action. He emphasizes the importance of love above all else and asserts that love is actually about the spiritual growth of another being. I absolutely *love* this idea. If we are considering the spiritual development of another human, we may have to entirely change our perception of what we consider to be loving because it's not just about us. If we are truly loving, we have to let go. And that is a true exercise in releasing codependency.

For instance, it would not be loving for a bird to prevent its chicks from leaving the nest. It is the bird's responsibility to guide its young until they are able to fly away on their own. If the bird never lets the chicks leave the nest, they won't learn to fly and ultimately won't survive. Similarly, if we don't encourage our children to grow, they may never thrive. Instead, they could stagnate and become emotionally stunted, never truly knowing who they are meant to be. Letting them go is love. Keeping them overly protected is codependency.

We want our children to grow and to know their worth and, as a result, reach their highest potential. Children believe in themselves when they witness us believing in them, accepting them, and loving them for all that they are. When a child knows they are loved, they also tend to feel valued. M. Scott Peck states:

> The feeling of being valuable . . . is essential to mental health and is a cornerstone of self-discipline. . . . [With] consistent parental love and caring throughout childhood, such fortunate children will enter adulthood not only with a deep internal sense of their own value but also with a deep internal sense of security.

I cannot stress enough to parents to always make sure their children truly know they are loved. Parents tend to assume, incorrectly, that their child just knows their parents love them. But many of my adolescent clients come in feeling like their parents are more concerned with their grades, their appearance, or any number of external factors (perfectionism) than with who they are. They feel their parents' desire to change who they are and how they act. They don't feel loved and respected . . . and their parents have no idea! The parent may be on a totally different page, thinking that pushing them to do well in school is loving. Or that taking them on vacation is loving. Or that telling them blue hair won't work in the real world is loving. These notions may be coming from the parents' idea of love (protection), but love is so much more than that.

UNCONDITIONAL LOVE VS. ENABLING

Unconditional love is often misunderstood. To unconditionally love someone means to love them regardless of their behavior. People may confuse this with enabling, which sends the message *You can do whatever you want, and I won't say anything about it.* Actually, people need to know that their behavior is not acceptable at times! But we can communicate this while also loving them unconditionally.

One of my clients expressed a time when he felt great love from his sister when she said to him, "I love you so much, but I can't let you be around me and my children if you are going to use drugs." This is love! We don't have to accept whatever people throw at us. Sometimes it's most loving to say, "I can't be around you right now because you're hurting yourself."

It's especially important to apply this concept to children because we do want them to feel unconditionally loved, but we don't want to enable them. Here are a few examples of loving statements that have strong boundaries against enabling:

- I love you, so I cannot buy cigarettes for you. If you smoke in the house, you also won't be able to live here.
- You don't need to go to college, but if you're going to live at home, you must have a job and pay rent. To help you get on your feet, I'll give you three months to find a job before I start charging you rent.
- I can't tell you not to date David. However, I am not OK with the way he treats you, and so he is not allowed in our home.

BOUNDARIES MUST BE FIRM

I want to reiterate that boundaries are important in all relationships. They let people know what we will accept and what we will not. As it's been said, we teach people how to treat us. Many of my clients struggle with this. You must be clear when you establish a boundary, as seen in the examples in the last section. You also need to outline the consequences for ignoring the boundary, such as "If you smoke in the house, *you won't be able to live here.*" Every time you need to create a boundary, do so in a clear and firm manner so there is no ambiguity.

Children are smart—they know how we operate and which buttons to push. For this reason, we must mean what we say. For example, the other day my daughter threw a tantrum at her grandparents' house. In that moment, I told her that if she didn't stop, we were going home, and I meant it. She didn't stop, so we packed up and left. It was important for her to see there were real consequences to her behavior and that the boundary I set was firm.

EXTERNAL STRUCTURE BEGETS INTERNAL STRUCTURE

As our children grow up, we want them to have some sense of structure they can impose on their lives. I often see adolescents transitioning into adulthood with a limited ability to create their own structure. They go from high school (high structure), to college (limited structure), to postcollege life (no structure), and have a difficult time implementing discipline in their lives. If they do not have a regular nine-to-five job to keep them in a set routine, they often struggle because they no longer have external structure and lack the skills to create it themselves.

If we can help our children by creating structure for them at a young age, they will be more likely to develop an internal sense of structure. The best way to impose structure as a parent is with predictability and firm boundaries. Predictability means your child generally knows what to expect, such as *Dad usually comes home for dinner. He needs a minute when he gets home to decompress and shower. When he's done, we all get together and eat and chat about our days.*

Life becomes unpredictable when they don't know what to expect at home, which is common in households with addiction and abuse. They don't know "which Dad" is going to walk through the door. Will he be drunk? Will he lash out at Mom because he had a bad day at work? Will we eat together, or will he go sit by himself and not speak to anyone while Mom and I sit quietly in the other room so as not to disturb him? This type of unpredictability contributes to a lack of structure and causes real stress for children.

Being predictable as a parent doesn't mean you can't also be spontaneous. Doing fun activities together spontaneously is a wonderful thing! Changing a schedule every now and then is not a problem. Problems arise when there is *no* sense of a regular day or of the predictability of the behaviors of caretakers.

In my own children, I've observed how structure helps them feel safe. Although we spend a lot of time at our extended family's homes, regardless of where we are, we always try to have a setup and routine that helps them know what to expect and feel comfortable. Dinner and bedtime happen around the same time. Bedtime still consists of brushing teeth, getting changed, and reading a story before we lie down. This helps them learn to be flexible in being out of the house, but also to expect a reliable routine. This offers stability and comfort.

Healthy boundaries are another way to form structure in a child's life. By not allowing them to simply do and get what they want all the time, they know where the limits are. The limits are predictable and consistent, and this is actually comforting to a child. If the limits are always changing, they will be more anxious about what's OK and what isn't and will have a hard time forming their own structure later in life.

REFLECTIVE EXERCISE

Sitting in a comfortable place with your journal, reflect on this: Are my boundaries clear and consistent? Have I stated them out loud to others in a way that makes them know exactly what I mean? Do I have trouble enforcing these boundaries? Why? What does it bring up for me? Do I get emotional when people push my boundaries? Identify what boundaries would look like and how you could help to be consistent and clear in your parenting. Use the book *Boundaries: When to Say Yes, How to Say No to Take Control of Your Life* by Cloud and Townsend (2017) for more help on this topic if needed.

CHAPTER 17

IS IT REALLY ALL ABOUT THEM?

One of the most common phrases I hear parents say when talking about what they do for their children is *Everything I do is for them.* Hearing this is like nails on a chalkboard for me. It is the epitome of a codependent outlook.

THEY DON'T OWE YOU ANYTHING

When we do for others at the expense of ourselves, we create resentments. We can even harbor resentments for our children for the sacrifices we feel we've had to make for them. But this isn't fair—your child never asked you to do this! YOU were the one who decided to bring them into the world and become a parent. If you catch yourself thinking, *After all I've done for you*

. . ., it's important to reframe your thinking and take responsibility for all you *choose* to do for your children

For example, when you have a young child, it's easy to fall into the trap of thinking that everything you do is simply all about them. And yes, when they are babies and toddlers, we have to do a lot for their health and well-being because they are completely dependent on us. This can lead to many frustrations, because it's tough to have someone completely dependent on you every minute of the day! It's understandable to have moments of exhaustion and even slight resentment, but remember that it was your choice to have the child in the first place. Try to shift your approach to do what's best for you while doing what's best for them whenever possible, so you don't feel like they are running the show.

One way that my husband and I do this is to plan our car trips around our kids' naps. It could be easy to say I'm doing that for them, since they love sleeping in the car, but the truth is, I'm doing it for me! I want them to nap and rest, and I also want to enjoy the peace and quiet while I'm driving. This isn't selfish; it's just for sanity purposes and has the added benefit of my children getting some much-needed rest. It's not selfish to also do things for ourselves. It's actually more selfish to believe our children are running our lives, when we always have free will!

Make all your decisions without strings attached. Your child doesn't owe you anything for the sacrifices you make. Be mindful of taking care of your own needs and not overextending yourself.

A similar statement parents love to make is *I'm doing this in your best interest.* If this is the case, be prepared to state what you believe your child's best interests are and WHY! Is it about them, or you? If you can easily identify how what you're doing helps the other person, you are most likely on the right track. If you cannot do this without bringing yourself into the outcome, it may be time to reexamine things. For example, *I'm not going to go out because my child gets anxious when I do.* Is it really in their best interest not to experience anxiety from separating from you, or is it you who is having anxiety *about their anxiety*?

> George was a wealthy man who had the means to travel anywhere in the world with his son, Marcus. He also wanted his son to be well-traveled and culturally diverse. (That's about him, not Marcus.) In these types of scenarios, parents often set an expectation that not only should the child enjoy the trip, but they should also appreciate it. And if they don't, then the parents feel resentful—after all, they spent all that money! But why should we assume our children will like what we like?
>
> What George does instead is tell his son, "I'd love to go on a trip with you. Pick anywhere on the globe you'd like to go and what you'd like to do on the trip, and I'll make it happen!" What I love about this is how George doesn't make assumptions that Marcus will enjoy exactly what George would plan. It also shows his son the amount of work that goes into planning a vacation. The outcome is that Marcus may actually appreciate their time together more since he had a say in it. (This technique can obviously be applied to more realistic budgets.)
>
> It's not that it's evil for us to say, *I think my kids would love a trip to Big Sur.* It's just that we are often presumptuous and our agendas for our children get in the way of our ability to be present and inclusive. We think we know what our children want or need or simply what they would enjoy, which leads us to make

decisions without asking them. But the truth is, we may plan a lovely vacation and they may not enjoy any of it. We have no control over that! But getting your children involved in the decision at least brings up more opportunities to feel connected and fulfilled. If you can't travel around the world, you can still do this with small everyday outings and decisions. Have fun with it!

GET RID OF YOUR AGENDA

Most parents gasp and become defensive when I tell them they need to get rid of their agenda for their child. Astonished, and maybe thinking I've lost it, they often say, *What???* Unfortunately, it's the truth! When we have an agenda, it means we have a desire for our child to be, do, or feel something. This usually doesn't come from a negative place, but it's still codependent, and the outcome is usually negative for both parent and child.

Our agendas hold our child to our own expectations of who we want them to be.

We all have agendas. They can range from simple to more complex. For instance, we want our child to graduate college so they can get a good job. Or we want them to break up with their boyfriend who isn't treating them kindly (in our opinion). I could go on and on with examples of our seemingly positive desires for our children.

> Sometimes an agenda can even be as simple as wanting our child to be happy.
>
> Ramona was a codependent client who had been working on herself for a couple of years. She came in

> one day expressing her concern over her daughter's way of coping with difficult feelings. She expressed to me that when her daughter got upset, she would sometimes remove herself and sit quietly for upwards of forty-five minutes. Ramona didn't like this and told her to "put a smile on." I told Ramona to drop her agenda (to get her daughter to smile and be happy) and honor her child for the way she was working through her difficult feelings.

Young children have a strong innate desire to please us. This is a normal developmental aspect in the early years of life. As parents, our goal should be to help them move from trying to please us (meeting our agenda) to learning to please themselves (understanding their own needs, desires, and intuitions). If they don't learn this skill, they may always look to make others happy at the expense of themselves and fall into the pit of codependency.

When we can remove our agenda from the conversation, we can actually listen. We become curious. We learn from our children. We're then able to open up deeper conversations in which we explore their thoughts and feelings, without a predetermined agenda about what needs to happen.

In the long run, our children will do whatever they want. Hopefully they won't do things out of reaction to us, by either trying to please us or trying to rebel against us. We want them to do what they want with their lives because it feels authentic for *them*. When children feel restricted by us and our needs, they are more likely to react in problematic ways. Again, we want to help our children make the best decisions for themselves. Then they can have more clarity in their ability to tap into their own great wisdom.

It's also important to remember that our children shouldn't be expected to always make the best decisions. None of us do! Making less-than-perfect decisions is how we learn and grow. Yes, it's uncomfortable to sit and watch someone go through something difficult and potentially painful, but remember, it may be the perfect lesson for them. Don't stunt your children's potential to grow in whatever direction they need.

RELEASING FEAR OF JUDGMENT

People will always have judgments about what we do, and if we learn to please others above ourselves, we will not be true to our own nature. We will not listen to our gut. We might not take risks, for fear of how other people will see us. I still find myself wondering, *What will people think?* I'm only human! But then I tell myself, *Oh wait, this is MY life.* When children learn to mold their decisions to their parents' agendas and expectations, they grow up to be much more concerned about what other people think, which can hold them back from following their true desires.

Recently, a friend in her late sixties was considering trying new churches to see if she connected more strongly with the Divine in a different place of worship. However, she was stopping herself from taking the steps to do so as a result of her fear of judgment and a fear that her husband or son would make fun of her desire to step out of the norm. Even worse, she worried that her long-deceased parents would be upset with her exploration. This fear was clearly a result of judgment she perceived early in her life. This example sheds light on the fact that we don't lose this fear over time. In fact, it often intensifies.

> **REFLECTIVE EXERCISE**
>
> Check in with yourself frequently when you are feeling tension in your relationship with your child. Ask yourself:
>
> - What is it I want for them right now?
> - If I let go of this, how might it feel for me?
> - How might it feel for them?
>
> How could it help your relationship to let go of your need for them to do or be a certain thing? Most often, it lightens things up. It's a big dynamic shift. If it's more important for you to have a better relationship with your child than for them to do something the way you want them to, there is your answer.

CHAPTER 18

BEING PERFECTLY IMPERFECT

We want our children to see us realistically, not as some contrived version of the "ideal parent" we hold in our minds. As humans, we are simply imperfect beings. If we embrace this as parents, we will also help our children do the same in their own lives. However, if we do not embrace this in ourselves, we'll send the message that people need to appear "perfect" to be OK.

We want our children to honor both their wonderful qualities as well as the ones that are far from perfect. Every human has flaws, and that is OK. In fact, it's more than OK: It's normal, and it keeps the world interesting. Carl Jung spoke often about the shadow self. The shadow is considered the part of ourselves that we are not in touch with or that we deny. It's our personal blind spot about who we are that has to do with parts of ourselves that we dislike and repress. Unfortunately, when we don't accept who we are—the good, the bad, and the ugly—it can lead to many mental health issues.

A lot of us perfectionists have a shadow imperfectionist, the part of ourselves that may be in complete opposition to our perfectionist ways. This leads to what's called projection, which is when we see a shadow part of ourselves in someone else, but instead of realizing that our judgment is about us, we make it about them. A good rule of thumb is that any time you're in judgment of someone else, it has to do with something about you. It could be an aspect of yourself you are consciously aware of or not, but a good thing to ask yourself is, *How am I that too?* or *How am I the opposite of that?* For example, you have a friend who gives up easily, and you find that you judge her to be cowardly. How are you also cowardly? Or are you so often the opposite extreme that maybe you could actually use some more cowardice but don't want to admit that?

The shadow is dangerous because it's sneaky. We don't realize it exists, and so we aren't in touch with our own projections. You will often see shadow aspects of yourself in your children. Your children are actually here to teach you about who *you* are, so use them to help get more clarity on *your* shadow. For example, one perfectionist mother I've worked with had a hard time accepting her son for his relaxed tendencies. He simply wasn't as rigid as her and didn't feel the need to appear a certain way to others. He left his room disorganized, wore dirty clothes, didn't get straight As, and didn't brush his hair regularly. This mother couldn't stand coming face to face with the part of herself she had long let go of in favor of perfectionism. Her son is actually here to teach her how to let go, relax, and stop being so concerned with appearance.

YOU ARE ENOUGH, AND SO ARE THEY!

This is probably one of the hardest truths to believe and live by: You are enough. If you have taken the time to read these pages, it means you are taking time to reflect on yourself as a parent. That is the most important thing of all! Being self-reflective—open to seeing yourself clearly and considering both your strengths and your areas for improvement and accepting yourself for who you are—is the greatest gift you can give to your child. Remember that this is very different from being self-critical. Take, for instance, the difference between these two statements:

> *I got really angry when Tommy wouldn't eat his dinner; I wonder what was so upsetting for me about that?* (Reflective)

> *I always get angry when Tommy doesn't eat. What's wrong with me?* (Critical)

When we believe in our worth as a person and as a parent, we treat ourselves more kindly. We also treat others more kindly, because we're not in competition with them. In this mindset, we understand that we're all trying to do our best. We aren't trying to meet some unrealistic standard we have placed on ourselves, and we don't place these standards on our children or anyone else.

Having children brings up tons of ways we can compare ourselves to others. We see other kids who are more advanced, better behaved, or seemingly more content. When we are in our egos, we use this information to put ourselves down, judging that we're not doing enough, that we're doing it wrong, and that our children should be different. But the only truth is, being who we are is enough. If we are taking the time to explore ourselves, that's the best we can give. It means we are open to the idea that we're not perfect. Again, parenting is NOT about being perfect. It's about being perfectly human and raising perfectly imperfect humans who have the confidence to thrive in the world.

Always remember, you are exactly the parent your child needs!

REFLECTIVE EXERCISE

Repeat the mantra: *I AM exactly who my child needs. I AM perfectly imperfect. I AM amazing. I AM wonderful. I AM caring. I AM a great parent!* Let yourself continue on with all the wonderful parts of who you are! Feel free to repeat this daily or as needed.

CHAPTER 19

PARENTING AS A SPIRITUAL ACT

I am a spiritually minded therapist, which means I tend to look at all situations through a spiritual lens. Before beginning to work on myself, I had little faith. I did not grow up in a religious household, and I was unsure of the place of a higher power in my life. Through some deep therapeutic work with my spiritual mentor, I was not only able to discover myself but also my higher power. I often refer to it as *the Universe* and *God* interchangeably. My clients often joke about my strong spiritual side, which I'm not shy about. If it doesn't resonate, you can just let it go, but hopefully you'll at least give some consideration to the following.

There is a long-held spiritual belief that our children actually choose their parents. This means that their souls know on some level that we are who they need in order to work on whatever it is they are meant to do in this lifetime. Believing that we are the right parent for them can help us find solace in our parenting journey. Think for a moment about your own life. Even (and most especially) if you've struggled with your own upbringing, ask yourself the following:

Why did I need these parents? What lessons have they taught me? How have they helped contribute to my growth?

For me, my parents put me on the journey to becoming a therapist. I come from a long line of people who have experienced a lot of pain, including generational trauma such as the Holocaust. I am the first one in my family to really work on myself therapeutically. I believe I picked this family to stop the cycle! It doesn't always feel good, but I wouldn't be a good therapist if I couldn't relate to the difficult experiences of many of my clients. Thankfully, through a lot of difficult work, I've moved from a mindset of being a victim of circumstance to feeling empowered by my early experiences.

Shefali Tsabary has a fantastic book called *The Conscious Parent: Transforming Ourselves, Empowering Our Children* (2010) that explores this subject in greater depth. The core idea is that our children can bring us so much growth if we let them. If we approach parenthood in an authoritarian manner, thinking it's our duty to tell our children simply what's right and wrong, we will be doing them and ourselves a major disservice. If we can understand and embrace the fact that our children are actually our spiritual teachers, we have a much better shot at being wonderful parents. Let's revisit the Native American proverb from the beginning of this book:

Remember that your children are not your own but are lent to you by the Creator.

Our children are sent here not only to learn from us, but more importantly so we can learn from them!

Both of my daughters teach me every day about so many aspects of life and of myself. Sometimes it's painful, and sometimes it's easy and beautiful. Children should bring us to the depths of our shadow self so that we can learn who we really are. My daughters push me to grow in a way that nothing else and no one else could. My kids bring me face to face with my imperfections as a parent and a human. They push me to let go of my agenda of how they should act, who they need to be, and how I want people to see them. They force me to enforce boundaries in a stronger way than I've ever had to do before. On every level, my children are exactly what I need in order to grow into the person and parent I'm meant to be.

We often stagnate when we aren't allowing ourselves to grow from the difficulties we're facing. We may even believe we shouldn't have to deal with these difficulties rather than accepting them as a natural part of life. Parenting is difficult as hell. There is no doubt about that. Lean into it all, the good and the bad, the joy and the pain, for your personal evolution.

As Wayne Dyer so aptly says:

"Change the way you look at things, and the things you look at change."

I hope this book has helped you look at parenting in a slightly new way—and that you find fulfillment within this shift in perspective.

ACKNOWLEDGMENTS

Special thanks:

To my loving husband, Phil, who has been my greatest support on this journey.

To my Warrior Women, who came along with me on this ride, especially Rita, Lauren, and Karla. Thank you for encouraging, supporting, and walking me through this process. Karla, I couldn't have gotten here without your love and guidance.

To my clients, who teach me so much and keep me inspired. Thank you for giving me the opportunity and blessing to be with you on your journey.

To my family—Mom and Dad—thank you for everything. And to Danielle, my big sister and a soul mate in this lifetime.

To Laura Lee and the Girl Friday Productions team for your guidance in helping me bring this book to fruition.

To Stephanie, my great mentor, who introduced me to my codependency and perfectionism. This book is for you.

And of course, to Nannie, the woman who taught me love. Thank you all.

BIBLIOGRAPHY

Beattie, Melody. *Codependent No More: How to Stop Controlling Others and Start Caring for Yourself.* Hazelden, 1986.

Bradshaw, John. *Home Coming: Reclaiming and Championing Your Inner Child.* Bantam, 1990.

Bretherton, I., and K. A. Munholland. "Internal Working Models in Attachment Relationships: A Construct Revisited." In *Handbook of Attachment*, Cassidy, J., and P. R. Shaver, eds. New York: Guilford Press, 1999.

Brown, Brené. *Daring Greatly: How the Courage to Be Vulnerable Transforms the Way We Live, Love, Parent, and Lead.* Avery, 2015.

Carroll, Lee, and Jan Tober. *The Indigo Children: The New Kids Have Arrived.* Hay House, Inc., 1999.

Cloud, Henry, and John Townsend. *Boundaries: When to Say Yes, How to Say No to Take Control of Your Life.* Zondervan, 2017.

Gilbert, Elizabeth. "The One Skill That Helps You Live a Happier Life," *O magazine*, oprah.com.

Jacobsen, T., and V. Hoffman. "Children's Attachment Representations: Longitudinal Relations to School Behaviour and Academic Competency in Middle Childhood and Adolescence." *Developmental Psychology, 33.*

Kobak, R. R., H. E. Cole, R. Ferenz-Gillies, W. W. Flemming, and W. Gamble. "Attachment and Emotional Regulation During Mother-Teen Problem-Solving. A Control Theory Analysis." *Child Development, 64.*

Larose, S., and A. Bernier. "Social Support Processes: Mediators of Attachment State of Mind and Adjustment in Later Late Adolescence." *Attachment and Human Development, 3.*

Mellody, Pia. *Facing Codependence; What It Is, Where It Comes From, How It Sabotages Our Lives.* HarperOne, 1989.

Miller, Claire Cain, and Jonah Engel Bromwich, "How Parents Are Robbing Their Children of Adulthood," *New York Times*, March 16, 2019.

Peck, M. Scott. *The Road Less Traveled, Timeless Edition: A New Psychology of Love, Traditional Values, and Spiritual Growth.* Touchstone, 2003.

Simplypsychology.org: Psychology Article for Students.

Substance Abuse and Mental Health Services Administration, Center for Mental Health Services Promotion and Prevention In Mental Health. "Strengthening Parenting and Enhancing

Child Resilience," DHHS Publication No. CMHS-SVP-0175. Rockville, MD: 2007.

Tsabary, Shefali. *The Conscious Parent: Transforming Ourselves, Empowering Our Children.* Namaste Publishing, 2010.

Walker, Pete. *Complex PTSD: From Surviving to Thriving: A Guide and Map for Recovering from Childhood Trauma.*

Williamson, Marianne. *A Return to Love: Reflections on the Principles of A Course in Miracles.* HarperCollins, 1992.

Wong, Daniel W., Kimberly R. Hall, Cheryl A. Justice, and Lucy Wong Hernandez. *Counseling Individuals through the Lifespan.* Sage Publishing, 2015.

The Codependent Perfectionist's Oracle Cards are here to provide you with insight, guidance, and support along your therapeutic journey. With the Universe as your guide, you can use these cards to gain greater understanding of yourself. If you struggle with codependency, perfectionism, or any other issue, this deck is for you. Find out more at www.alanacarvalho.com.

ABOUT THE AUTHOR

Alana Carvalho is a licensed mental health counselor who maintains a private practice in New York City. Before founding her own private practice and cofounding Intuitive Healing Psychotherapy Practice, Alana held the role of site director at an outpatient substance abuse treatment facility. Alana supervises and mentors therapists in training. She has also been a lecturer on child development at the College of Staten Island and has worked with hundreds of people and their families on healing patterns of codependency and perfectionism. Alana has a podcast called *The Codependent Perfectionist*, where she discusses a variety of relationship issues connected with codependency and perfectionism.

For more information on codependency, perfectionism, The Codependent Perfectionist's Oracle Cards, or Alana's online support group, and to listen to *The Codependent Perfectionist* podcast, visit alanacarvalho.com.

www.ingramcontent.com/pod-product-compliance
Lightning Source LLC
Chambersburg PA
CBHW071344080526
44587CB00017B/2955